CORNERS

VOICES ON CHANGE

AMY LOU JENKINS

JACK
WALKER PRESS

Copyright © 2018 by Jack Walker Press
All rights reserved.

No part of this publication may be reproduced, stored in a retrieval system, or transmitted in any form or by any means, electronic, mechanical, photocopying, recording, scanning, or otherwise, without the prior written permission of the author and copyright holder. Exception: One or two sentences may be quoted for review purposes.

Limit of Liability/Disclaimer of Warranty: This publication is sold with the understanding that neither the author nor the publisher is engaged in rendering legal, investment, accounting or other professional services. While the publisher and author have used their best efforts in preparing this book, they make no representations or warranties with respect to the accuracy or completeness of the contents of this book and specifically disclaim any implied warranties of merchantability or fitness for a particular purpose. No warranty may be created or extended by sales representatives or written sales materials. Neither the publisher nor the author shall be liable for any loss of profit or any other commercial damages, including but not limited to special, incidental, consequential, personal, or other damages.

Every effort has been made to trace the ownership of all copyrighted material included in this book. Any errors that may have occurred are inadvertent and will be corrected in subsequent editions, provided notification is sent to the publisher.

Some names and identifying details of people described in this book have been altered to protect their privacy.

Reprinted material has been noted where known. Any copyright indications elsewhere in this book are an extension of this copyright page.

Corners
Voices on Change
Edited by Amy Lou Jenkins
Literary Collections/ Essays 2. Biography & Autobiography/Personal Memoirs
3.Family and Relationships/ Prejudice 4. Family & Relationships

Jack Walker Press.com
Mukwonago, WI

*Dedicated to the writers of room 212 who studied with me at UW
Madison's Continuing Studies Write by the Lake
and to their generosity to the reader
and in celebration of their voices.*

CONTENTS

Introduction	vii
1. Intersection of Then and Now	1
2. Shooting a Deer	9
3. Choosing My Religion	14
4. I Became a Mother But Lost Myself	25
5. Echo	30
6. Gracious Living	36
7. Playing at Racism	43
8. Cherry	46
9. Yesterday's Home	50
10. The Ceremony	59
11. Caught	66
12. Codependence, Anxiety and a Smack on the Head	74
13. Take That, Doormat	79
14. Can You See Me Now?	85
15. Minutes of the Meeting	89
16. I'm Sorry	94
17. Suffering Migraines	97
18. Electing to Love	103
19. Seeing Through Mohammed's Eyes	111
20. Lemon and Love on Crete	117
21. Whom to Love	123
22. One Too Many Graves	127
23. Once Upon a Spa	136
24. Ah ha ha	143
25. Baila Conmigo	152
The Authors	161
About Jack Walker Press	169

INTRODUCTION

Amy Lou Jenkins

Change comes, but I try to stop it. Change and time move together. I've tried meditation to be in the moment—to stop time. Sit still, observe the thoughts go by. Try not to judge the thoughts. Perhaps I've attained stillness for a few moments, but sitting meditation doesn't work for me. I don't have the discipline to clear my head, and the whole idea of being in the moment is weird because as soon as I have the experience of being in the moment, I'm thinking—

"That moment is gone, am I in the next one?"

Watch that thought go by. "Now I'm thinking again. Oh crap."

"When's the last time I got my teeth cleaned? I'm paying for that dental insurance. I should go. Remember that beautiful young woman in Florida who got AIDS from her dentist in the early 90's. She died. Her dentist infected her on purpose. Oh great, try not to judge that."

Watch the thoughts go by.

Nothing.

"I did it—I cleared my mind."

"Crap I'm thinking about my cleared mind."

Every moment of an attempt to *be still* is in motion. The Earth spins on its axis at about a thousand miles an hour. The electrons in the hydrogen atoms in my body spin at about 4.8 million miles per second. I don't sit still: I don't stay the same, not ever.

I can do a walking meditation. If I hear a pileated woodpecker, I go still and can focus in the direction of the drumming or the "wuk wuk wuk" without thinking too much about the smears on the stovetop that I should wash off before my Mom comes over. The spear of the Dutch iris is swollen with purple edges of tomorrow's blossom, those petals laboring at escape. A walking stick insect eats its own shed skin. I am observing and don't feel movement away from the time and place. The moment is still passing. It finishes. I have to stand up. My back hurts.

I can't get through a friggin moment in the moment. Yet, I do find comfort in ritual. The Sun comes up. My children are beautiful. The moon's phases follow their pattern. Spring can be wicked, but it comes. Aunts make potato salad. Mama Mia's tops lasagna with a lot of mozzarella cheese. Our neighbor serves every brandy old fashioned—sweet, with three Queen olives (yum). Cold beer tastes good with pizza. Fred Astaire dances with drums in the annual viewing of "Easter Parade." Reading in my comfortable chair feels luxurious. My sister walks with me. I think my spouse can see my beauty, even though I can't. I still have one parent. Birthdays come to prod celebration of existence. We do make progress, learn a language, play the flute. We march to call attention to national problems. We get a promotion, save for a house, finish the remodeling, build a life, save a life. We always move away from our birth date. Move toward something else. Spouses leave. Employers "let" us go. Politicians lie. The other side gets it wrong. We change our minds or refuse to change them despite mounting evidence. Disappointments come. Pets die. People die.

Perhaps I failed at meditation because I want *being in the moment* to stop time. To stop the pull of gravity on my eyelids, to prevent the heart disease from hurting my Aunties, to keep the dog playful. To keep the car from falling apart. To stop the CO_2 level from rising in our atmosphere. No rhinos killed today. No forest cleared. No cancer cells invade. Seven-year-olds still giggle when Grandpa burps. My eyes can still see the depth of dark teal just before the end of dusk. What good is it to think of nothing, while the things I love disintegrate or move beyond me?

The voices who tell their stories don't quell my desire to dig my nails into time and try to drag the changes to a stop like a locomotive on a short track. I can't make those sparks fly. I can read and be with the voices who tell their tales and live their moments of clarity, pain, and comfort. Their voices are important. I can witness the grace possible while moving through change as the world spins beneath our feet and our atoms vibrate and twirl.

I think there is no actual *in the moment,* unless I stop believing in moments as static. Maybe our whole lives are a moment to a greater consciousness. Perhaps, when consciousness can back away from thoughts of self, when we trace another's thoughts as they puzzle their way through the labyrinth of making sense of inconsistency, we can glimpse the worth of their struggle, their humanity, and their noble walk through change. Our noble walk through change. And perhaps that is what it is to be alive.

ONE

INTERSECTION OF THEN AND NOW

Julia Anne Miller

On a peaceful May morning, at a quiet intersection in a still-sleeping part of town, a man in a truck ran a red light and changed my world.

I recall very little about the accident itself. I am driving slowly through the intersection, attention focused forward, wanting to be certain the lady across from me, whose left turn signal is flashing, recognizes my intention to go straight. It seems we are the only two people up and about, except for the driver and kids on the school bus my son has just boarded. There is a stunning slam of something hard against my head and left side, loud yet muted, and for the slightest fraction of a second, I know I've been hit by another car, and instinctively pull my tiny dog, who is sleeping on my lap, against my chest, then a woman's voice, then a man's, and a slow realization that things are different. Days later, I will remember what the voices are saying: "I saw you! You ran the light!" "Oh, my God, I didn't see her! I didn't see her!"

People are outside my car, trying to open the door, shouting. My head is pounding, like a harsh heartbeat. The female voice, from afar: "You've been in an accident. EMS is on the way. They're on their way. What's your name, honey?" I'm confused and say nothing. I think time passes. Sirens, then my door is making a terrible sound. A person is kneeling next to me, telling me to remain still, but I'm not moving. My dog, Willie, is removed from where I am still holding him against my chest. He is limp but alive. Later, his hair will gray in the exact pattern of how I am holding him. His personality will never be the same, but neither will mine. I am lifted into the air, then I'm in a moving vehicle, strapped flat. My left side shakes uncontrollably. I try to stop it because it hurts, but I can't. I am so cold. Someone is talking to me, keeps talking. I'm in a bright hallway, moving quickly, the ceiling rushing past, and still the talking, talking, someone asking me questions. I know I'm in the emergency room, but it's moving so quickly, there are so many people. I'm asked my birthday. I get it wrong. I get the year wrong as well, give a last name I haven't used in decades.

The lights are too bright. I am in a strange fog. A screen of flickering white covers my vision, like an off-the-air old-fashioned television screen. My daughter and son-in-law are facing me, my brother is wearing the same purple polo shirt as the doctor. Time passes. We are told there is no internal bleeding, nothing is broken. But my sacral lumbar region, at the base of my spine, is swelling, a concern because a disc is malformed, leaving my spinal cord unprotected. On my left side, my sinuses are damaged, my septum deviated, a molar displaced, and my face, upper back, shoulder, hip, knee, and ankle are still swelling and bruising. Bright spider webs of light cross my visual field. No breaks, no bleeding. I want to go home and check on Willie. He must be completely traumatized. I am to return if my thinking and vision don't begin to clear within eight hours and see my doctor within 48 hours even if they do. I agree, then promptly forget. I am confused and disoriented but happily leave with my family. When I stand up from the wheelchair at the emergency room exit, my pelvis dislocates. The life I know now begins.

It begins mostly alone in my apartment for five days because my daughter is in labor and there's no one to check on me. My care is in the hands of two teenage boys who do not yet drive, cannot grocery shop or cook. They don't know how to help me. I don't know how to ask. Awkward and embarrassed, they take turns listening for me to fall in the bathroom. At the five-day mark, I can't move due to head pain, and the doctor sends a taxi to pick me up.

It continues with eight hours of physical therapy per week for six weeks. The first day, my shoulder slips out of place. Neuromuscular electrical stimulation to reduce muscle spasms and pain, and ultrasound therapy to treat deep bruising are administered at each session. There is pain when moving, pain when still.

I take Willie outside three times a day, slowly descending and climbing the stairs leading to my apartment. I am dizzy and off balance, but Willie will let no one else near him. At first, we just step onto the grass. After a couple of weeks, we can walk half a block and back. I am determined for my life to be as normal as possible. I keep waiting for my head to clear.

Double vision and light patterns last for two weeks, followed by sensitivity to light. When my light tolerance gets worse in the fall, I visit my ophthalmologist of fifteen years. I explain my head injury, ask if my eyes are damaged. My eyes are healthy, he says. With his best attempt at hiding his shock at my intellectual decline, and somehow managing to not sound condescending, he suggests sunglasses. He explains that the light has changed because leaves have fallen from the trees. He adds I could also wear hats with brims that would shade my eyes. These things have not occurred to me.

I cannot make a grocery list. I cannot count. I cannot understand storylines on television shows. I watch the same movie five times in the first two weeks, trying to remember the plot, but each time, parts of the story are new. I think it is morning all day, most days, probably because I feel like I just woke up after a restless night and need coffee. Apparently, I state this exact feeling several times a day, every day. I pay the same bills twice in one day, a couple of different days. I try to order a pizza online, get frustrated and cry, too loud and too long. My teenage sons sit on the couch beside me, bewildered. They are as powerless as I am. There is nothing they can do.

For the first month, I cannot comprehend what I read. When I reach the end of a paragraph, I have forgotten the beginning. I never regain the ability to read directions or descriptions of unfamiliar processes.

I forget that my granddaughter is left handed. I forget being in the delivery room when she was born. I forget to turn off the stove. I forget to use a potholder to remove hot pans from the oven. I forget I am cooking and leave the kitchen. I forget to close the front door. I forget to put on shoes when I leave the house. I forget I've said the same thing over and over. I forget, I forget, I forget.

Sometimes I cry when something is funny, laugh at heartbreaking news. If I make a phone call, I stutter, then lose the correct order of words. I can no longer understand spoken instructions. When people laugh after speaking, I have no idea what's funny. Why won't my head clear?

My daughter looks at me with fear in her eyes. She is all efficiency and nonchalance, believing she can mask it. The doctor says give it six weeks, then eight weeks, then three months, six, nine, a year, and then stops saying anything.

Rehabilitation therapy seems endless as months pass. They teach me how to organize my clothes to get dressed, to fix my hair in a simple style. It's too difficult so I cut it. I learn to navigate the perimeter of the grocery store. Therapists caution me to avoid loud places, bright places, places with more than one person talking. I don't consistently recall their lessons.

My visual memory resets every few seconds. I cannot retain information long enough for it to be stored in my short-term memory. I cannot transfer simple information from one piece of paper to another. For months, I can go nowhere unfamiliar alone. I enter a room for the first time over and over. Unfamiliar faces are new, then new, then new again. Simple directions are frustrating and hard. Step one, then step two, then...what was step one?

My left side develops a mind of its own. I walk into stationary objects, fall, and stumble on my left, live with a dozen bruises, nicks, and scratches. I veer to the left when walking, following a terrain that appears wavy and uneven. I don't know it yet, but I have a neurological blind spot on my left and have lost depth vision. I have a small permanent bruise on my left cheekbone to complement my slight left-side facial droop. I struggle to complete tasks with my left hand. I concentrate hard, but it shakes and ignores my intentions. I open the oven door with my right hand and pour dinner directly inside with my left, as if it's the most natural thing in the world. I knock dishes off counters. I drop, rather than place, glasses onto the table. My hand twitches and I fling food. I am a terrible dinner date.

I don't like to look at pictures of the baking and furniture projects I once loved. I feel loss and sadness, but mostly I mourn being able to remember what it felt like to enjoy them.

After fourteen months have passed, my neurological tests are repeated—four hours, then three more. The damage is determined to be primarily in the area that affects vision, visual memory and processing, and visual-spatial relationships. There is likely damage in the corpus callosum, the band assisting communication between the frontal lobes, as well. Some of my right brain functions are in the $<1^{st}$ to 10th percentile. My left brain is in better shape, but there are odd spots of diminished ability. I am told that things have improved as much as they will. My brain is askew. I learn to be lopsided.

I am referred to a neuro-ophthalmologist for several more hours of testing because my neuropsychologist says I become "stimulus-bound by objects in the left visual field." The new doctor discovers the blind spot in my left eye. The left refuses to work in tandem with the right. I have difficulty tracking objects. My eye is perfectly healthy and capable of vision, but my brain doesn't acknowledge that parts of my left side exist. My brain "neglects the left." I can't tell because my left brain automatically creates its own substitutes for the missing parts of my visual field, and tells me I see everything. I am completely confused by this information. I *believe* my brain: I see everything, perceive the world not partially, but completely. Even now, I can't really understand this. How can I be partially blind and not know it? I want to understand what I am not seeing.

When I return to work as a library page, putting things in alphabetical and numerical order, over and over, for twenty hours per week, I find the repetition and predictability soothing. The state Office for Vocational Rehabilitation teaches me to keep a card with the alphabet close at hand, but I still confuse L with P and put S before R. Sometimes I alphabetize in reverse order. I know the order of numbers, but at times there's a disconnect between that knowledge and the ability to put them correctly in sequence.

Over time, I learn that if I initiate conversation, I can usually control it, but I might pause mid-sentence and have trouble starting back up. I stutter when I least expect it. I forget the names of objects and describe them instead: "that flat thing where people sit and eat food." I randomly substitute words that start with the same letter. I will always remember when I took a very long time to figure out how to hang three pictures. I finally succeed, and proudly record in my journal that I hung three potatoes on the wall.

I find I have difficulty answering unanticipated direct questions. Even if I know the answer, I can't immediately find it. My doctor likens it to a computer trying to load. The circle spins and spins. Approximately two minutes later, long after the conversation has moved on, the answer finds me. Or I might give an answer that is unrelated to the question without realizing it until later, if at all.

I no longer understand humor and metaphors. My brain translates the words literally. I grow confused or begin to carry out actions that were intended as a joke. It makes for awkward social interactions.

Throughout my navigation of life with a traumatic brain injury, I maintain the ability to write. It saves me. When I cannot clearly speak my thoughts, or engage in spoken conversation in a meaningful way, when I can't risk saying the wrong thing on a sensitive subject, I can sit at my keyboard and write. I can write out long responses to anticipated questions for unavoidable social settings, then practice speaking them out loud.

When I finally realize my head is not going to clear, my essential human nature kicks in and begins my life story anew. When the process of restoration starts, I find myself nearly unrecognizable. I don't remember who I was, nor do I know who I am.

I record my days on paper. I write poetry. As my ability to read returns, I write about what I am reading. The process of writing begins to bring me back to myself. She's a new self, and I don't know her intuitively yet. She confuses me, but I am learning to live with her.

Looking in the mirror, it is hard not to feel the jolt of an old and a new self. I am bound by my unhappy relationship with the reflection I see—the slight fall to the left side of my face, the tiny bruise on my cheekbone, the diminished animation and downward slant of the left side of my mouth.

It's important to grieve, to mourn the loss of who I was. It has been a very concrete process for me, through months of testing, cognitive therapy, trial and error, and learning ways to work around my neurological deficits. It has also been a vague, dream-like awareness that something is gone.

It is equally important to accept parts of my brain simply can't work. Every day when I pull into my parking spot at home, I count on my fingers how long it has been since Willie has been outside. I have a difficult time with details, and can't remember the month, the day of the week, the ages of my grandchildren. I write the wrong words when making notes and writing lists. I find odd, incoherent sentences written in a loose hand on pieces of paper throughout my house. I have no idea what I meant to say.

But I remind myself to go ahead and dance to the sometimes-discordant music I now hear. The rhythm has changed, and it slips off into strange riffs, but it still has a melody of sorts. The notes will continue to become more familiar over time. I decide to celebrate my birthday on the day of the accident, May 13, the day my new self was born.

TWO

SHOOTING A DEER

Amy Lou Jenkins

He's not really my uncle, but I call him Uncle Bill. He's been my Aunt Lil's boyfriend for a dozen years. Bill is a carpenter, mason, electrician, and hunter. Hard of hearing, he just starts up a-talkin' about what's on his mind rather than responding to a conversation. "She come up from the swamp and raised her nose in the air. Arrow pierced her heart; she went down quick."

He chewed swamp-doe venison sausage while he talked. My up-north Wisconsin relatives spend their November vacations and weekends in the swamps and fields of northeastern Wisconsin. The meat is important to their winter diet, so all are thankful that the chronic wasting disease that has infected other parts of the state's deer population, has not been found in Marinette County. My relatives wouldn't starve without the venison, but the hunt, the freezers and mason jars of venison steaks and roasts, and the recipes for cooking the lean protein are essential to the up-north culture. Our German and English ancestors came to this land based on the promise of land, game, and a kind of freedom that feels related to what goes on between humanity and the forest.

When I was a young girl, my parents made perennial November drives from Milwaukee to the land where my Mother had hunted and dogged every autumn in her memory. When I was about nine, they taught me to dog; I never carried a gun but helped the hunters with my little-girl squeal. Relatives who knew the terrain chose a square of land. Eight to ten of us, dogs and hunters alike got in line, yelping and stomping to flush out deer, while other hunters stood in watchful wait.

The woods were cold, but my belly was warm with eggs, hash browns, and fried ham and bacon. We even ate apple pie. Since it was Grandpa's breakfast favorite and apples were easy to find on abandoned land that had once been farmed by families, everyone got a pass to eat pie with eggs. Along with parents and grandparents, aunts, uncles, cousins, and hunting pals, we all gorged on a big old farm breakfast. These folks were bonded by their familiarity with 4 a.m. farm mornings, and the hunt further bonded the group as providers of meat for the family. In our family, the men and women hunted, and that was also a source of pride for me. That kitchen was wood-stove warm, smelled of coffee and fried bacon, and rattled with the chatter of hunting plans. They used specialized words I didn't understand.

"If we drive the Spikehorn, Evie can use her old stand—where she shot the eight- point year before last."

"The road off the Long Slide's been showing activity."

"You using the 30 ought 6, or going back to the McMillan?"

They sounded competent and excited, chewin' and fast talkin' at the yellow aluminum-edged table.

Before daybreak, we were in the swamp. Walking through plots of November swampland was toe-numbing cold. Sometimes the swamp water crusted with a skin of ice that broke when I stepped on it. Each step brought a moment of security, then a two-inch, or six-inch, or even eight-inch plunge into chilly swamp water. I always worried my foot would go ten-foot deep, and I'd be screaming and going under like a quicksand victim, and they'd all think 'What a good dog she is; wow what a screamer.'

Those hunters weren't worried. Even though I usually couldn't see them, an adult on each side of me tracked my pace on the line. They wouldn't let me get a step ahead. They knew the land, woods, and names of the trees, birds, rocks, moss, and animal tracks. I loved being in the woods, the realm of my relatives. I loved the stories at the end of the drive about who had seen what, the foxes, hares, pileateds and other exotics that had escaped my gaze. Often, they'd ask if I'd seen the young doe, old buck, or fox that passed in front of me. No, I generally only noticed my feet as I struggled through the rough terrain.

On a later drive, after it began to snow, watching my feet evolved into watching for animal tracks. I recognized rabbit tracks, followed by what Grandpa later confirmed were bobcat tracks. Both sets of tracks grew further apart, and I understood I was following the chase, and I was a part of the chase. The bobcat tracks disappeared many feet before the creek, echoing a deathblow pounce. In the middle of a small stream, a snow-covered boulder held a pool of fresh, bright blood, and one set of tracks leading away. My nine-year-old self imagined a dead bunny, yet I couldn't deny the excitement of being so close to the pursuit. I imagined that bobcat, the soft white-spotted fur, the three soft pads of the paws moving silently through the swamp and woodland. I was working to make peace with the small scene before me. I began to appreciate the beauty in the blood on the snow when I noticed our entire dog line had halted. Mom, twenty yards to my left, made crossing-guard arms to me; the message—stand still.

I saw him, his shiny brown eyes, his moist nose that rose up from the ground and twitched before he turned his ten-point rack away from me and darted. The shot detonated my stillness. Everyone starting moving, and I got the arm wave to pick up my pace.

I thought they missed him because he ran and leapt into my view three more times before he dropped. We followed the blood trail. The shooter yelled from up ahead. "He's a beauty." I caught up to the hustle and stories of the kill. They posed with him, took pictures, and pulled up his head by the rack so I could see how he'd have looked lying on the forest floor listening for danger.

He was beautiful.

He was dead.

I stood in the background of the scene and watched them cut into his belly, release the steaming warmth that had been life, and pull the slippery red and blue entrails out onto the frozen woodland. Snot and tears froze to my face. I have always remembered that scene, and how confusing and sad it was to see those details of life and death.

I never dogged with the hunters again, always found excuses, spent my Novembers in the city, never graduated from dog to hunter. I just couldn't watch, couldn't yell, and couldn't shoot.

With his mouth full of swamp doe, Uncle Bill had evoked images of that hunting kill, and I refused a slice of venison sausage, perched on a Ritz, for emotional rather than logical reasons. Uncle Bill chomped as he left the kitchen to bring in more firewood.

Uncle Bill had bought forty acres of land with money he earned from decades of skilled manual labor. He cleared a section of forest to build a cabin from the very trees he'd cut. At over seventy-five years old, he did it all himself. He felled each tree and hauled the logs to the sawmill and back. He nailed each nail, ran the electricity, and laid the stone fireplace. Although he had Aunt Lil select the arrangement of the green, beige, blue and grey stones, citing "What the hell do I know about color coordination."

Uncle Bill took us all out to the almost finished cabin on our most recent up-north trip. About twenty-five relatives were there; all the local families were hunters. All were February festive without a holiday to celebrate: cooking, playing games, sledding, taking the kids on snowmobile rides, making a racket of jokes, laughing at the baby giggle, and teasing each other. Aunt Lil told about the unfinished ceiling. "Bill laid pine boards on the floors and walls. He was going to lay them on the ceiling, but I told him he might have too much to drink, and not know where to walk.

We were a noisy bunch, except at one window that faced a field. "Look." Five-year-old Abbey's finger pointed out the window, and her small voice and stillness hushed us. Five deer moved slowly toward tan piles in the snow. A quiet voice behind me explained. "Bill feeds them hay and corn." By this late in winter, food's scarce. Lots of deer don't make it through the long winters. He's got names for the regulars. He even picked up a glass storm door from the dump and put it on the outhouse, so he can watch them from where he sits after morning coffee.

The day and evening stayed fun and noisy, but everyone took at least one turn at the quiet window. These deer and venison lovers have an honest relationship with their prey. I glimpsed it before we ate our potluck dinner.

Asking God to "bless our food" changed meaning for me. I always thought it was about me, like "Thanks for feeding me" or "Don't let this food give me gastritis," or even "Let it nourish me, so I might serve you." I never understood the direct meaning of "bless our food, like my up-north relatives do. They understand the sacrifice of the deer.

THREE
CHOOSING MY RELIGION

Duane L. Herrmann

I was 17. I had just left home to attend college in Topeka, Kansas, the closest city with a university. A year earlier my father had been killed as a result of a tractor accident. I had grown up on a farm but did not want to farm.

I was interested in religion, but not the church I had been raised in. I had attended Sunday School there every week since a toddler, was confirmed, taught Sunday School and ushered all four years of high school, was President of the youth group and wrote the children's Christmas program in my Junior and Senior years. The church recruited me to be a minister, but I couldn't accept major concepts of the theology.

One of the church constitution assertions was that at some unspecified time after death, our decomposed bodies would float out of their graves into the sky, then be magically changed from a physical to a spiritual body when Christ returned. That didn't make sense. How could the molecules which had been part of any decomposed body be reassembled to be that same body again? How could those physical elements obtain the ability to float into space when they couldn't do so when alive? But, if this reassembled physical body was going to be changed into an eternal, spiritual body, why would it be reassembled in order to be changed? Why would the physical body be involved at all? This process of resurrection involved only the soul. Bodily resurrection made no sense. It wasn't necessary.

I also could not stomach the idea that anyone who did not anticipate Christ before His appearance or accept Him in that church's way, was condemned to Hell forever. That made no sense. There was no way for countless billions to have any idea of Christ. For the All-Loving Creator to condemn them for something that was beyond their control, would be cruel and fickle. I could not accept that as an attribute of God.

Away from home, I could explore other religious beliefs, one of which was the Bahá'í Faith. I had been invited to an informal gathering called a 'fireside.' The speaker had just returned from non-combatant duty in Vietnam where undeclared war was raging. He told of several miraculous events involving himself and others there.

In addition to the stories, I was impressed by an experience I had as I approached the home where it was held. Dusk was approaching , so interior lights in the neighborhood were on. I saw that light as well as a different kind of light from the windows of the house I was going to. There seemed to be rays of golden energy pouring out of the windows and open door. I didn't know what that energy was, but I knew it was good, and I wanted it in my life. This was something I could never explain to my family. I was not aware at the time of the subjective nature of apparent miracles in the Bahá'í Faith. Miracles are not dismissed, because they do occur, but their value is to the one who witnesses them, not to others. This vision was sufficient indication to me of something important to attend to.

After my own study of this religion with the Bible, I realized that the Bahá'í teachings fit more closely to my personal beliefs and the Bible than did those of my family church or any of the other churches —and I joined the Bahá'ís. My family was outraged and bewildered:

What had gone wrong? How could I abandon the church? How could I turn my back on God? How had they failed? How could I have been so misled?

As a result, I began to feel unwelcome at gatherings of my extended family. I was nearly kicked out of one home at Easter, and my cousins were separated from contact with me. I was also warned against corrupting my siblings. As the oldest in my generation, they see my potential influence as dangerous.

I had heard of stories of other Bahá'ís who had experienced rejection because of their decision, so I was not surprised but, this presented a dilemma. The main aim of the Bahá'í Faith is to create unity, and here, my acceptance was the cause of disunity. I knew not to argue (arguing is forbidden for Bahá'ís) or oppose them. The only course of action I could see was to demonstrate my love and value for my family. I would continue to visit and be kind and polite and demonstrate that they were still important to me and that I valued being part of the family. If they did not want to know anything about the Bahá'í Faith, though I was excited to share my discovery, I would not tell them.

For many years there was an uneasy relationship. No one asked why I made the change, or what Bahá'í beliefs were, and I did not force the subject. Family members did lament that I was taking my children to Hell with me, and they were such nice children. I offered to pray for them if they wanted to pray for me. That was a surprise, but the offer was accepted.

Once, I was asked if I was afraid to die.

"No!" I so want to. It will be wonderful. But, there are things I need to do here, first. I don't get to choose the time of my death."

That answer calmed some fears and paved the way for other, easier discussions.

"Do you believe in God?"

"The Creative, Sustaining Force of the Universe?" I asked in return. "Yes, certainly."

"Do you believe in Jesus?"

"The Son of God who sacrificed His life for the redemption of mankind? Yes." Those answers also brought incredible relief.

Gradually, over decades, various members of my family relaxed to different degrees. One uncle stayed home from church one Sunday to watch a CBS produced documentary on the Bahá'í religion. An aunt offered to watch my baby when I had to go out of town for a weekend meeting and my wife had to work. Another aunt admired the good family I was starting. One grandmother talked to her sister and relayed to me her assessment that, "Bahá'ís are a good people."

My other grandmother, the one who had taken me to church every Sunday, offered food she had grown and picked from her garden. She offered it for "your people." That gift signaled a kind of acceptance. Once, she sat with me and looked at every page of a book which surveyed events and accomplishments of the Bahá'í community around the world. She was impressed that there were Bahá'ís in all countries, cultures, and costumes, and most significantly, that they were a happy people. When we came to the photograph of the Bahá'í House of Worship which had been destroyed by Soviet authorities, she was outraged. How dare anyone do that to a building that was important to these people, and her grandson! What was important to me had now become important to her.

Nine years after the death of my father, I held a private memorial service for him, inviting only my two brothers. Our sister lived too far away to attend. Afterward, my middle brother asked me questions about Bahá'í as he tried to understand my decision to change faiths. I answered him as best I could. He didn't say another word about it. A year later, on the tenth anniversary, I held another memorial, and the two came. Afterward, my middle brother said that he, too, wanted to be Bahá'í.

I was astonished. We had not spoken of it all year! I had no objection, but the family did! I was obviously a corrupting influence, taking him to Hell with me, and was no longer welcome in the homes where my cousins were still growing up. The separation was so definite now that my aunts began to hold private birthday parties for my grandfather – no cousins, just my brothers and myself and our families.

I continued my efforts to demonstrate love. A few years later, when my aunts began to clean out my grandparent's home, they found letters to their grandfather, my great-grandfather, from family in Germany, written in German. No one had known the letters existed. They were translated and, for the very first time, the rest of us learned about our German relatives. The aunts gave my brothers and me a copy of the English translation.

I was so excited about the contents of these letters that I used them to write a little family history storybook. I printed it and bound it with a special cover. On the cover, I used a photograph from distant relatives who had just "found" us. That branch of the family had moved to Oregon, from South Dakota, over half a century before and lost touch. The photograph was of my grandfather and his parents. Grandfather was an infant in his fathers arms, his mother alongside in front of their tiny house in the 1890s.

When I presented this to my grandfather, he was speechless. He was just a simple farmer, with little formal schooling, and never imagined anyone would do such a thing for him. My aunts and uncles were amazed too. Just before it was printed, one of my aunts made contact with a relative in Germany. The return letter invited us to visit. I closed the book with that invitation. When it was printed, I sent them a copy.

Five years later, and after my grandfather died, I was able to accept that invitation.

"Your book came today," I was told as I got off the train in Germany where the family was waiting. I was mystified. I then learned that a cousin there had paid to have the little book translated and then had copies printed for the family. I was amazed.

"Ich schreibe dieses?" I asked. I wrote this?

"Yes." I was told by one who spoke English. His expression said, why would you doubt that?

"In Deutsch?" I asked in mock surprise.

"Ja. Ja," he answered laughing, now that he got the joke. I was now a German author and an esteemed member of the family. The family there knew nothing about their American relatives and, I was surprised to find out, they knew little of their family that had been related in the letters. That little book gave them the history of both sides of their family. I was amazed and grateful that I had been able to return to them their own stories.

Before the trip, I had contacted Bahá'ís in the area, and one came to visit while I was there. She was a native Australian who had married a German and was fluent. She offered to translate for us. My cousin would tell her a story, she would tell me in English, and I would write it down while my cousin told her more. From this, I learned much more family history. The German relatives were amazed that I would know someone in their country when I had never been there before. They could not comprehend the connections which bring Bahá'ís together. My Germany family was so impressed that the translator was invited to stay for supper. The translator, in turn, was impressed with the invitation. It was not typical German behavior to invite a virtual stranger to a meal in the home, at a restaurant maybe, but not a home.

So, what is this connection that would cause an American to contact strangers in a foreign land to ask to meet them and a foreigner of another country in that land to respond?

It is part of the unifying process which members of the Bahá'í Faith are enacting and creating around the world. For the entire life of the religion, ordinary members have left their homes, traveled and settled in other cities or countries to share the Message of Bahá'u'lláh: that the human race is one race, that there is only one Creator, that our Creator has progressively educated humanity through special Messengers, and now is time for people to set aside war and work together to build a human civilization of peace where everyone can benefit, grow and flourish.

This is a religion with no clergy, no rituals, and no exclusion of others. In fact, Bahá'ís don't even have a term for those who are not Bahá'í. No one has a label of "outsider." No one is outside the human race.

Bahá'u'lláh taught that our Creator progressively educates humanity through a series of Messengers, individuals who overwhelmingly manifest attributes of God. These Messengers, or Manifestations, include among others: Abraham, Moses, Krishna, Zoroaster, Buddha, Christ, Muhammad and, today Bahá'u'lláh. This process will continue into the future as long as humanity exists.

Bahá'u'lláh affirmed that the purpose of this physical life is to prepare for our next stage of existence after death. The degree of our preparation is reflected in our actions. All Manifestations have taught us to be kind to others, and the circle of "others" has gradually expanded from the family to the tribe, to the city, to the nation and, now, the whole earth. It is imperative that we recognize all fellow humans as equal heirs to the planet and human civilization, or we may well self-destruct. And, who will benefit from that? No one.

For these teachings, and the heretical proposition that women are equal to men, Bahá'u'lláh was exiled and imprisoned. The last forty years of his life were spent in political confinement of one kind or another. His extensive properties were seized, and the family was reduced to poverty. He was exiled from His native Persia, now Iran, to the Ottoman Empire. There He was exiled successively from Baghdad to Constantinople, to Adrianople and, finally, to the penal colony of Akka, which today is in Israel. During this time two of his sons died for lack of medical care, all of the family suffered severe privations.

Bahá'u'lláh's Message has been adopted by more and more millions around the world who are building new lives and communities. They are offering to share these teachings with their family, friends, colleagues, and neighbors. They are teaching children moral and ethical virtues, empowering youth to become active in improving society and strengthening families. They are offering hands of friendship across all kinds of boundaries which divide people, building bridges encouraging people to find common cause and work together.

After a survey, in the 1980s, the World Christian Encyclopedia stated that the Bahá'í Faith was the second most wide-spread religion in the world. This was accomplished in less than two centuries. No other religion has spread so far, so rapidly, so suddenly. People from all backgrounds have found something in this way of life that resounds in their hearts. Since that time national Bahá'í communities were revived or formed in Russia and all other territories of the former Soviet Union and Eastern Europe.

One of the teachings which continues to amaze and excite me is about the human soul. Bahá'u'lláh presented a continuum of life which has a simple, coherent flow of process and development which makes a great deal of sense to me. He explained that the life force goes through various stages of existence with its own spirit: first the mineral realm, then vegetable, then animal, then human. At human conception the soul becomes individualized. The human soul is connected to, but not contained in, the developing fetus. The fetus develops the physical attributes necessary for life in this physical world.

During life in this physical world, the same process is repeated, though on a higher level. In this physical life, we are to develop spiritual attributes necessary to function in the next, spiritual world. This life is our preparation for the next. Bahá'u'lláh stated that at the time of death each soul will learn of the value of its life on earth and each will be given a spiritual form best suited to its immortality.

This correlates with what I saw in dreams. In one, I saw my grandparents who had both died some time before. Granma said to Granpa that I would not recognize them. While she said this, she jabbed him in the side with her elbow, a signature gesture of hers.

"You have the same faces!" I exclaimed with joy and love. They seemed to be oddly dressed, but I didn't give another thought to that.

Later, in the next scene of the dream, I glanced out and saw the two of them, very contentedly, hovering over and tending flowers. The "clothes" they had on were actually very large wings wrapped around their bodies. Granma loved flowers and taught me as a little boy to love and care for them too. Granpa simply loved Granma. What I saw made perfect sense.

Our spiritual progress will continue through more realms than just the one after this life. The progress can be endless, ever advancing closer to the Creator, the source of our life and being.

This sequence of continual progression was not proposed by a philosopher after deep thought. It came from a princely noble with little formal education. Bahá'u'lláh, the Prophet-Founder of the Bahá'í Faith was born in 1817 into Persian aristocracy, descended from Keturah, the third wife, of Abraham. Bahá'u'lláh's education consisted of calligraphy, horsemanship, and archery. He became attracted to the teachings of a religious reformer and was arrested for that association and suspicion of involvement in a plot to assassinate the Shah. At His trial Bahá'u'lláh was found innocent, therefore he could not be executed as His enemies wished, so His wealth was stripped, and He and His family were exiled from the country forever.

None of these calamities would have happened to Bahá'u'lláh and His family if not for His claims of revelation. Bahá'u'lláh repeated what He had explained in His Tablet to the Shah of Persia, "O king! I was but a man like others, asleep upon My couch, when lo, the breezes of the All-Glorious were wafted over Me and taught Me the knowledge of all that hath been. This thing is not from Me, but from One Who is Almighty and All-Knowing."* If He merely denied his claims all the worldly trappings would have been restored to Him. He gained no benefit from His actions.

In answering questions posed to Him and spontaneous Revelations, Bahá'u'lláh revealed some 40,000 texts. Some are as short brief prayers, others are expositions of thousands of words. One subject covered in these Writings, unlike earlier religions, is the manner in which the community of His followers is to be organized. Bahá'u'lláh outlined a system of councils at various social levels. He described their functions, responsibilities, and limits. And, He appointed a successor, one to head the religion after Him. This successor was 'Abdu'l-Bahá (1844-1921). Bahá'u'lláh made acceptance of Him identical with acceptance of Himself. These provisions are considered the Bahá'í Covenant. This covenant has prevented the Bahá'í Faith from being split. Attempts have been made, but none have succeeded in establishing a rival branch of the religion.

'Abdu'l-Bahá, in His Will and Testament, created the office of Guardian and appointed Shoghi Effendi Rabbani (1897-1957) to fill the position. He, too, made acceptance of the Guardian congruent with acceptance of Himself. This was a further development of the Bahá'í Covenant. This may seem complicated, and the names are unfamiliar, but these provisions have given the religion a stability and a focus that others don't have. It places the focus not on personalities, but on principle. This changes everything.

Shoghi Effendi made it his life's work to prepare for the creation of the international council ordained by Bahá'u'lláh. He did this by guiding the international spread of the religion with the establishment of local and national administrative councils. This international council was elected in 1963 with the title: Universal House of Justice. It is the Head of the Bahá'í Faith now with its Seat at the Bahá'í World Center in Haifa, Israel, just across the bay from Akka, Bahá'u'lláh's final prison. Oddly, this location of the World Center, because of the actions of Ottoman authorities nearly two centuries ago, is now used to justify persecution of Bahá'ís today in Iran. Because some financial contributions are sent to the World Center, they are accused of supporting Zionism. Muslims, on the other hand, who contribute financially to Muslim holy places in Jerusalem are, oddly, not accused of Zionism.

One responsibility of the House of Justice is to gather, preserve, collate, translate and publish the Writings of Bahá'u'lláh as well as guide and administer the affairs of the Bahá'í world community. It provides guidance for a grass-roots movement to transform society. More and more people every day are attracted to this process of transformation. It brings together people from all levels of society, giving them common cause to work together for the betterment of all. Diverse types of people unite within the Bahá'í world community in a scope that has never happened before in the history of the human race.

While my son was serving at the Bahá'í World Center, I went to visit him. I offered to volunteer during the day while he was occupied with his responsibilities. This meant I was a temporary member of the staff. I was able to see the World Center functioning from the inside. People there came from all over the world. They didn't wear labels, but their skin coloring was an indicator. The hues were more varied than I was used to seeing at home, in Kansas. There were rainbow shades of brown, plus white, yellow and red. The entire human race seemed to converge.

I could see that people all over the world were traveling the same path as myself, trying to put into practice the teachings of Bahá'u'lláh, and to work together to create new social patterns. If this is the future of the human race, I do not mind my difficulties. I am content.

---

* Bahá'u'lláh, *Epistle to the Son of the Wolf*, p.11

FOUR
I BECAME A MOTHER BUT LOST MYSELF

Cate Dicharry

I am thoroughbred for motherlove. My father and mother are each one of eight children, in the case of my maternal grandmother, eight children amid 12 pregnancies. In the case of her sister, my maternal great-aunt, one biological child followed by seven miscarriages, several at full-term, and, eventually, two adoptions. I have three brothers and 51 first cousins. There are twins in every generation, on both sides of my family. The women in my bloodline carry, bear, and love their children with greed and verve. They are unapologetic and full in motherhood.

I am no different. I have always known I would want children. Four, five, six children. All the noise and enmeshment of immediate family.

When I became pregnant, I thought I had an idea of what motherlove would do to me, what it would feel like to adore my baby. I'd been on the receiving end for 31 years, after all.

During pregnancy, I did what I could to prepare for the substantial difficulties of motherhood. I read about sleep training, about how my son's circadian rhythm would mismatch my own so that he'd be wakeful, likely crying, for long stretches of night. I learned of the real possibility I'd defecate during labor and composed a lengthy apology, just in case. I studied techniques for breastfeeding with an inverted nipple. I read comedy-as-coping-mechanism essays telling me my infant-tyrant would drive me to drink, that motherhood would drain me of time, emotion, and energy, unlike anything I'd ever experienced.

That it would be grueling but that the moments of joy would be blissful and pure.

I was also deeply concerned with the ongoing debate over maternity and contemporary feminism (à la Marissa Mayer, Anne-Marie Slaughter, Sheryl Sandburg, and the innumerable responses and arguments), and how I should arrange my life as a self-respecting feminist and ambitious writer/mother.

My son is now 10-months old. The difficulty of motherhood, it turns out, lies not in the logistics—manageable, or at least endurable, are the sleepless nights, breast infections, teething tantrums, untreatable infant congestion, naptime blitzkrieg—neither in feminist posturing which, in the heat of maternity, strikes me as impersonal and irrelevant. No, it is motherlove that, as my husband says, pummels me. Nothing I read or heard prepared me for what it feels like to live with love at this high a decibel. Nobody explained what it would do to me.

Many writers have captured aspects of motherlove. Hope Edelman calls it "a love so sudden and huge you [don't] know how to make it fit."

Emily Rapp's dragon-hearted motherlove is "without limits or expectations...a love that left people speechless, confused, and delirious with misunderstanding."

Cheryl Strayed wrote of her own mother, "We were her kids, her comrades, the end of her and the beginning."

Motherlove is not a series of momentary bursts of joy, and it is not an abstraction. It is constant and material. It is obsession. I want my son. I want him all the time. I want to be physically with him, preferably holding, touching and/or kissing him but I'll accept being in the same room, watching him play or babble or crawl or wail. When I am not with him, I think of him and ache. I don't mean "ache" in a romantic, hyperbolic way. I mean corporeal discomfort. Fidgety, inattentive, slightly nauseous, pins-and-needles restless. I want him.

All the time.

And I am afraid in motherlove. I worry over my son growing into a child, a teen, a man, having to make choices and mistakes, feeling confusion, anger, sorrow, regret. I dread his heartbreak. I pre-mourn his future injuries, illnesses, and death. These thoughts, the daymares of the loving, are nearly intolerable.

My son made a home inside my body for nine months, and his first worldly contact was with my chest. His existence transformed every part of me: breasts, hips, stomach, hands, ass, vagina, brain. Every day we see one another naked, unabashed. I've gone to the bathroom with him on my lap. Nursed him on a crowded airplane. Ingested his saliva, sweat, and urine. Studied his irises and wondered if they are my husband's or mine. I have held him as he slept. Ours is, by far, the most intimate relationship I have ever had. To call it codependent would be an obscene understatement.

How strange that as this joy and intimacy fill my life, I am hounded by loss.

I was a reader and writer before I became a mother, but in the past year, I've read only five books. I am too ashamed to quantify the very few words I've written. And yet when I have the opportunity to make the practical choice to focus on something else—reading, writing, staring out a window, anything other than my son—I cannot do it.

It's not guilt over being apart from him, nor is it an issue of control; I don't always need to be the one caring for him. I am not a practitioner of attachment parenting, and I am not an especially overprotective or nervous mother.

It's not that I need more "me time"—to take an afternoon and get a pedicure, or shop for clothes that flatter my postpartum figure. It's not about time at all. I have a loving, supportive partner with a flexible work schedule. I can easily carve out the hours.

It's partly the standard-issue baby-shaped hole in my brain, but mostly I cannot work because I find my son literally irresistible. I cannot not want him, not choose him, his presence, his baby song, his little baby body. I choose him, over everything else, every time.

Now, after nearly a year of making that choice, day in and day out, there is nothing left of me. I am no longer a reader, no longer a writer. No longer a feminist. There is nothing there but motherlove. I am consumed. I have lost my selfhood. *The state or quality of being an individual, particularly of being a person separate from other persons and possessing his or her own needs or goals.*

The self. The essential being. The substantial nature of a person.

And so within the tremendous joy of motherlove, I am unhappy. As unhappy as I have ever been. Incomplete. Flaccid. I knew motherhood would change me, but I am too changed. I am unrecognizable.

I am not saying I suffer. I am not saying, how terrible for me, loving my healthy beautiful son so very very much. I am saying simply, this is what it feels like to be lost.

My circumstance is both extraordinary and banal. Few mothers have the time and egocentricity to indulge in contemplations of selfhood. Then again, every single day selfhood is lost by any number of people through all manner of diversion. Alcohol, video games, haute couture, sex, grief, body weight.

It fits then that the language containing the essence of motherlove belongs to addicts detailing addiction. Stripped bare by shame and loss, many addicts write without sentimentality or fear of vulnerability. Theirs is the language of destruction and paralysis and weakness and need. It contains the rare combination of truly heavenly highs and crushing, hollowing lows. In this language I find comfort.

For David Carr, "to be an addict is to be something of a cognitive acrobat. You spread versions of yourself around, giving each person the truth he or she needs—you need, actually—to keep them at a remove."

This describes who I've become in motherlove. Most days I play a false version of my true depleted self, keeping others at a distance, saying only what is expected from a new mother: "I'm thrilled, it's amazing, so amazing, such an incredible journey, I'm loving every second of it." This is the lie of omission I tell again and again and again. To friends, family. To my father, my mother. My husband.

The trouble is motherlove knows no moderation, and there is no rehabilitation. Instead, it requires deliberate, hard-won restraint.

Because no person, certainly no infant, should be forced to bear the burden of obliterative love. My son didn't create this situation, I did. He is a victim, not an accomplice. He deserves better. He deserves the fuller, happier version of his mother. His mother the reader. The writer. The feminist.

And so I am tasked: to reclaim focus and brainpower and, somehow, forge the will to put them to work. To choose creative, intellectual engagement over my son. To opt out of a morning of play and fuss and wonky crawling and instead sit alone in a quiet room and write fiction. To finally, if only for a short time, want something else, some piece of myself, as much as I want my own child.

How I became a mother but lost myself was previously published June 24, 2013, at Role Reboot: Life, Offscript.

FIVE

ECHO

DEBRAH SCHMEDEMANN

We were not supposed to meet this way. No: we were supposed to meet at this newborn's home. My daughter, Mary, and her husband, Adam, had explored all of the birthing options available on the north side of Chicago for an unremarkable first pregnancy. Mary, nearly thirty-one, healthy and confident, skittish about the trappings of modern medicine, chose a home delivery, assisted by a doula and midwife.

But the baby had a surprise: a breech presentation—too complex for a home delivery—discovered after five hours of hard labor in the waning moments of July 3rd, 2015. An ambulance rushed Mary (panting through her contractions) and Adam to the nearest hospital. Mary was whisked into the surgical delivery suite, as Adam donned the required scrubs outside. By chance, an old-school obstetrician was on duty that night. Rather than perform the expected surgery, he attended as Mary pushed out her baby boy into the doctor's hands amidst the bright lights and cool clamor of the surgical suite—not, as Mary and Adam had hoped, into the hands of his father amidst the low lights and calm warmth of their living room. From the other side of the delivery room doors, Adam heard Mary's grunts and the baby's squawks, and he gave thanks.

Adam then sent a text to my husband Craig's phone, received about three miles away in our condo. We were half awake already. We had been with Mary and Adam earlier that evening as labor started, so we were on alert. Firecrackers had begun sounding all around Chicago on July 4th beginning a moment past midnight. To our ears, they crackled for Luke Bowmann Arents, 8 pounds 7 ounces, 21 inches, born at 1:39 a.m.

So it was that Luke and I first met in the maternity ward of Swedish Covenant Hospital. By then it was about 11:00 a.m., and he had spent his first night and morning snuggling with his mother and father—as well as being pricked and prodded and washed and weighed and diapered by all those hospital people.

Walking towards the hospital room, I realized that I had never imagined this moment. I do have a good imagination; indeed, I had imagined Mary, my first-born daughter, for a dozen years before she actually came to be. And I had a premonition about Luke's conception right about the time he was conceived. But my mothering imagination has always been stuck at the point when my own mother's experience ended: she lived only until my sister and I were teenagers. So I had never considered what it would be like to see my two daughters come of age, begin careers, or marry, much less bear children.

Thus unprepared, I stood in the doorway and took in Mary sitting in the hospital bed, wearing a dark robe from home, her hair in a messy bun. She held a lump of new life swaddled in a blanket of white cotton printed with blue lions, his pink head resting against her bared breastbone. It felt like my heart skipped a beat. I knew, of course, that a baby had been in there; the last month or so, her coltish figure had sported a bump so big I had worried it would burst. I was sure her bump was much, much bigger than my two baby-bumps had ever been. Indeed Luke was bigger than my two newborn baby girls. Of course, this natural athlete daughter of mine, who ate so well and meditated so calmly and did yoga as labor started, would deliver a breech baby in just a few contractions her first time out!

And yet, a boy? This I had to see. As one of two sisters and the mother of two daughters, my half-serious motto had always been, "I don't do boys."

When Mary handed Luke off to me, my gaze focused on his rounded rosy head, capped in delicate brown strands. His big eyes peered blue-brown and unflinching. His nose commanded attention. My first comment about the new love of my life: "Gee, he has a really big nose." His pouty lower lip looked like a tulip petal. His shoulders and arms were clothed in delicate brown strands (Adam: "he's a beast!"), and his pink hands curled loosely into fists. He was alert as could be, rested still against my chest, and conveyed a mix of disgruntlement and curiosity. His torso was swaddled to protect and conceal his bruised baby-boy parts.

I flashed back to when I first saw Mary. The dozen years I had spent imagining Mary began shortly after my mother died. Her death came suddenly (the result of a cerebral hemorrhage), painless for her but a shock for her family. Within days, I sought continuity by resolving to have a daughter to carry forth my mother's middle name. As the years went by, I developed a picture of "Mary" at birth, as a toddler, as a child, as a teen. Yet when she was born, Mary looked nothing like the infant image in my mind's eye—a dash of disappointment. The pang passed when I realized that I had given birth to an actual Mary, and I fell hard for the baby I held in my arms.

And now, thirty-one years later, I held Mary's baby Luke: a boy baby, a baby I had never imagined, and yet, as I looked at him, I felt I had known *him* all my life.

The next day was Sunday. My husband Craig and I did not want to go to Mary and Adam's church and risk revealing the news of Luke's birth—Mary and Adam should have that privilege. Ravenswood United Church of Christ was within an easy walking distance, so we found ourselves there.

To my mixed-Christian self (born to parents with Baptist and

Lutheran roots, baptized by an Episcopalian Army chaplain, raised Presbyterian, married to a one-time United Church of Christ minister), this sanctuary was familiar space. Beams stained deep walnut crisscrossed its high, white-washed ceiling. The pews of well-worn oak flanked a rose-patterned carpet. The sun filtered through stained-glass windows of familiar New Testament scenes and a painting at the front depicted yet another. Two ranks of organ pipes framed the altar, into which was carved "Heilig Heilig"—"Holy, Holy, Holy" in German (the language of my forbearers).

The service began. We settled into our pews, into the still and warm air, into the liturgy celebrating our nation's birthday under God. I heard familiar scriptures, listened to familiar themes in the sermon and sang familiar verses. "Our country 'tis of thee, sweet land of liberty." I rose in accord with the asterisks in the bulletin. As the service neared its end, the organ heralded a familiar tune, and the congregation rose to sing the Battle Hymn of the Republic: "Mine eyes have seen the glory of the coming of the Lord . . . . " But I froze as the hymn, my father's favorite, began. Still, I sat as I heard—for the first time since his death two years earlier—my father's rich baritone singing "the glory of the coming of the Lord," over my right shoulder.

I don't know when it was first said of my father that he had a "colonel's voice." In 1941, a twenty-three-year-old Keith Schmedemann entered the U.S. Army as a second lieutenant; he retired a full colonel in 1969. During World War II, he landed at Normandy Beach the day after D-Day, fought through the Battle of the Bulge, and contributed to the liberation of the Jewish internment camp at Buchenwald. He went on to lead a battalion during the Korean Conflict. During my early childhood, he commanded an infantry battle group in West Germany during the Cold War; my family was called back from a trip to Berlin just before the wall went up. Stateside, he spent several tours of duty in the belly of the Pentagon.

I remember hearing his colonel's voice many times as I sat in the chapel in my childhood church. My father was the superintendent of the church school. He would stand before us and deliver a children's message—a ramrod straight and trim man just over six feet tall, attired in a tasteful grey or blue suit, crisp white shirt, and striped tie; bald already in his forties with soft brown eyes. When we children were restless or rambunctious or rowdy, my father would call out "Children!" in his colonel's voice, and we would settle down in a flash. His was a voice of calming authority.

I remember hearing his colonel's voice, in 1968, when the nation upheaved in riots over racial and economic injustice. Famous and unknown people were dying; my family watched the television news; my father drove me and my sister to the outskirts of the areas of anger and anguish in Washington, D.C. I was fascinated, appalled, scared. And my father's voiced our responsibilities to make the country better. His word choices were cautious and mild. His message was a moral imperative.

I treasured hearing his voice when he and I sat side by side in a pew and the time came to recite the Lord's Prayer. After my mother had died and his second wife as well, my father would take my hand, and we would recite the prayer together using the traditional "Our Father" phrasing.

So what was the essence of my father's colonel's voice? As I became a law professor and then a mother, as I sought to find my own authority, moral direction, resolve, and faith, I pondered this. I used to think it had something to do with dropping his pitch and rounding the tone. But then I listened to him speak about opening the gates of Buchenwald and learning what he saw there (testimony he recorded for the Holocaust Museum in Washington, D.C.), and I realized the colonel's voice has nothing to do with sound. Rather it is an echo of the life lived, the experiences embedded, the lessons learned.

This is why that hymn I heard sung the morning after Luke was born—the Battle Hymn—is meant for my father's rich baritone. "Mine eyes have seen the glory of the coming of the Lord. He is trampling out the vineyards where the grapes of wrath are stored. . . . Glory, glory hallelujah."

Mary and Adam had chosen not to know the gender of their unborn child until its birth. About two months before Luke's birth, when I was jogging, two intuitions about my future grandchild came to me. The boy intuition was the stronger. That baby boy, I sensed, would be born on July 4th, and his parents would name him Luke or perhaps Keith.

Keith was a rational prediction. Mary and her grandfather had adored each other. As he died, it was Mary who held my father's right hand, as I stroked his cheek, while his family prayed the Lord's Prayer around him. Adam and my father were buddies during the few years they knew each other.

I have no idea how I guessed that Mary and Adam would choose the name Luke. Other than being a Biblical name, it has no particular significance to either family. Mary and Adam simply liked the name for its own sake. In Greek, it means "light-giving."

Luke and his great-grandfather may have different names and may not live during the same years, yet they are as otherwise connected as two people can be—through the genes of Keith that have passed through me and through Mary to Luke, through the experiences that molded Keith, informed me, and shaped Mary and will now carry through to Luke. As I saw in Luke's face the moment we met, and as my father's voice that Sunday morning gently let me know, Luke does not need to carry the name Keith to bear witness to my father's lineage. And I hope that I do not need the full measure of a colonel's voice to evoke the echo of my father.

SIX
GRACIOUS LIVING

Charlotte Mitchell Smith

I pulled the salt and pepper shakers from the second shelf of the dining room buffet and handed them to my brother Tom. With their pink roses scrambling over white bone china, they were my favorites and a pair my paternal grandmother had brought with her when she came to live with us. I thought the shakers would look pretty on the table Tom and I were setting that night. The dinner was to be a special one for my grandmother and her daughter and son-in-law, my Aunt Evelyn and Uncle Sterling, on the last night of Evelyn and Sterling's stay with us. Besides, to forget to use fancy salt and pepper shakers when company was coming was to risk our mother's rebuke. Tom and I once tried to excuse their absence by complaining, "Nobody uses them. Why do we need them?"

Our mother's reply was swift. "We believe in gracious living."

Her remark was a frequent refrain of my childhood, but my mother never defined her term. Tom and I learned its meaning from what my mother asked of us and what she did. Her greatest lesson came during that dinner in 1961 when I chose my favorite salt and pepper shakers for the table. A decade later, I would learn another lesson.

By 1961, when I was fourteen and Tom was ten, we had learned the basics of my mother's rules. We knew we would eat in the dining room each Sunday noon and each night, except on Thursdays when my father went to Kiwanis and on Saturdays when we ate hamburgers or hotdogs in the kitchen. From our daily chore of table setting, we learned what went on the table each night and the hierarchy of silver and china that each meal and occasion required. Most nights, we put out stainless steel and white ironstone. Colorful Fiesta ware stayed in the kitchen. Sterling silver and wedding china were reserved for dinner parties, holidays, and birthdays. Each summer, Tom and I helped our mother remove all the dishes, glasses, and silverware from the dining room buffet, wash and polish them, and put them back on dusted shelves, a task we had finished just before Evelyn and Sterling had arrived for their biennial visit to see my grandmother.

As Tom placed the salt and pepper shakers on the table, my father returned home with my aunt, uncle, and grandmother. Through the open front door, I watched the four of them walk up the sidewalk onto the screened porch and into the house, slowed to a mosey by the late day heat. After the hot car ride, Sterling's and my father's shirts clung to their backs, but their ties remained knotted around their necks. The short sleeves of their shirts and their lack of jackets were the only concessions they had made to Iowa's humidity. The muggy air warned of a thunderstorm before dark.

Despite the pulling down of window shades, the closing up of draperies and the opening up of both again in a rotation that followed the passage of the sun around the house, the dining room had stayed hot. Water droplets condensed on the sides of the filled ice tea glasses on the table and dripped down to leave small puddles on their coasters.

Tom and I waited behind our chairs for the others to come in. The regular seating disrupted by our guests, Tom had been moved to my side of the table with Uncle Sterling between us and my grandmother and aunt across from us in Tom's usual place. The table set, dinner ready, and all present, my parents sat down, as normal, at each end of the table.

Uncle Sterling pulled out the chair for my aunt. "Here you are, Miss Evelyn."

Sterling's southern vowels, foreign to our Midwestern roots, rolled round through his mouth like butterscotch candies melting into syrup. With the military stride of the Virginia Military Institute graduate and World War II captain he had been, Sterling walked around the table and pulled out my chair.

"There you go, Miss Charlotte."

After grace and the passing of food, the adults began to talk about Evelyn and Sterling's recent move to a city apartment in Washington, D.C. Sterling had taken a new job there as treasurer at a private day school, a more prestigious position than his previous job at a military boarding school—and his high school alma mater—on the Eastern Shore of his native Maryland.

"Does traffic keep you awake at night?" my mother asked and then glanced out the window at darkening clouds. She pushed her short brown bangs further up her forehead where glistening drops of perspiration gathered.

"Yes, ma'am," Sterling answered. "Washington cars are noisy, noisy, noisy."

Sterling's comment piqued the interest of my driving-loving father. "I didn't notice that last summer."

"Definitely so. The District is full of Negroes who don't keep their cars up."

"Sterling," my aunt's rayon dress rustled when she leaned forward in her chair, "I'm not sure—"

Uncle Sterling interrupted her, "Now, Miss Evelyn, you know they don't."

Jabbing his knife in the air, Sterling turned to my father. "And the way those niggers drive."

I sat up straight. Had I heard right? I heard Tom's fork clatter down on his plate. He must have heard that word, too. We both would get our mouths washed out with soap if we used it.

"Those fool niggers," Sterling's voice grew louder and his words rapid-fire. "They just rev up their motors, race their cars down the street and load 'em up full of darkies."

Darkies? I knew the word from watching jerky black and white films of minstrel shows, but I'd never heard it used in conversation. Was it right to call people that? My father looked down, away from Sterling, and stacked his mushrooms in neat piles on the side of his plate. My grandmother sat still, not eating, shrinking smaller in the white lacy cardigan she wore despite the heat.

"I don't think those niggers have the brains to keep their cars on the right side of the road," Sterling continued.

I heard that word again and then the drumming of my mother's fingers on the tabletop, the sound muffled by the table pad and white linen cloth. No one else spoke, but Sterling went on.

"It's a wonder there aren't more accidents. That would sure take care of those coons."

The muggy air grew heavier and still; breathing, harder and slower. My father coughed. He looked at the ceiling. Suddenly and at the same moment, my mother and father stood up, dinner plates in hand. Had Tom and I missed my mother's signal to clear the dishes? We hadn't finished eating.

My mother reached across Tom's place and snatched up Sterling's plate. Without a word, my parents left the room. Without his food, his audience diminished, Uncle Sterling fell quiet.

At the kitchen door, my mother turned, stared at me, and then at Tom. We stood up, cleared the remaining plates, and followed our parents into the kitchen. In silence, the four of us cleaned and stacked the dishes. Then booms of thunder sent us scrambling off to close doors and windows before pelting streaks of rain blew in.

Although my brother and I had learned our mother's lessons well and set a pretty table for our guests, my parents' silent rebuke of Sterling taught us that gracious living was more than what we put on the table before us. Our family never spoke of Sterling's outburst nor much about the Civil Rights Movement of the sixties, so I never knew for sure what drove my parents to stand up in objection to his behavior. I always sensed that some standard of decency and respect for others had been so far breached—even if those others might never gather at our table—that my parents couldn't passively accept the ignorant hate, nor could they verbally respond. Perhaps verbal confrontation wasn't gracious.

Sterling and Evelyn continued their biennial visits to Iowa, we visited them occasionally, and they came back for my wedding. Sterling did not erupt again, but like river pilots ever alert to underwater dangers, my parents steered all conversations away from topics likely to trigger another explosion.

After we married, my husband Mike and I moved to North Carolina for graduate school. During a January semester break, we decided to visit Sterling and Evelyn, then living in Dover, Delaware, where Evelyn taught school music, and Sterling was a state accountant. I fidgeted in the car as we neared Dover. Mike had met Evelyn and Sterling briefly at our wedding, but this would be his first long visit with them, with any of my aunts and uncles, for that matter. What if Sterling spoke as he did on the night of the storm? What would Mike think of him, of Evelyn or my father, of me?

That evening, while Mike and I talked with Sterling in the living room, I watched Evelyn set the dining room table with her wedding silver, china, and crystal. As my mother had taught Tom and me, Evelyn nudged each knife, fork, and spoon into alignment with the edges of the dinner plates and wiped each crystal glass with a soft towel to remove all smudges.

I took a cautious glance at Sterling. He seemed much the same as always. He still wore gold-rimmed glasses and still slicked back his hair without a part, though now the pale skin of his scalp showed through his thinning and graying hair.

After a few moments of conversation, Sterling waved towards a ranch house across the street. Wondering why he waved, I looked out the picture window more closely and saw a woman bend over to help a child out of a car. The house looked like any other in the subdivision. Yet, Sterling called it to our attention. "She's a teacher at Miss Evelyn's school," Sterling said.

The woman held the child's arm as she guided him up the snowy driveway. I sat straight up in my chair. The mother and child were black.

"Oh, no," I thought, "here he goes again."

Sterling leaned forward and jabbed his finger toward the woman. "We have other families like that in the neighborhood, now."

I braced against my chair. "Please," I willed him, "don't say anything more."

Sterling pointed across the street again. "That boy there."

I glanced at Mike to catch his attention, hoping to warn him with my look.

"Hemophiliac, often bleeds, always in the hospital," Sterling said.

Mike shifted his position. Sterling paused, then said, "Good family, though. They take good care of that boy. I sure feel sorry for them."

Sterling settled back in his chair. "I remember back home once, they found a black man drowned in the pond. Worst case of suicide ever, the sheriff said. Couldn't have been, of course. His hands were chained behind his back."

Mike scuffed his feet against the carpet. I rubbed the palms of my hands down the rough fabric on the arms of my chair.

Sterling closed his eyes for a moment before he spoke. "No one said anything, of course." He opened his eyes and turned toward me. "Wasn't right. I see that now."

Sterling rested his head against the cushion back of his chair and closed his eyes again. I exhaled, not aware I had been holding my breath. Neither Mike nor I spoke. Outside, snow continued to fall, hushing the passing cars into silence. The late afternoon light grew dimmer, the grayness darkening. The quiet stillness edged inside and lingered in the corners of the living room for a few moments until Mike and Sterling began to speak of winter snow and icy roads.

So startled by the contrast between the sympathy and regret that Sterling expressed that night and the vitriol of his speech ten years earlier, I did not ask Sterling how or why his attitude had changed. Or perhaps, I had learned not to speak of such things.

Although I wrote Sterling's words as truthfully as I can remember them, they were hard for me to write. They are as offensive written as they were spoken. Even Sterling's admission of past wrongs, as genuine as it was, came embedded in a cruel and standard joke about the Ku Klux Klan and lynchings, a joke I won't repeat. Yet, it is important for me to remember the story of his words. On a hot summer night in Iowa, my parents' abrupt action in ending dinner—and Sterling's words—taught me the duty of acting against hatred and bigotry. On a quiet winter night ten years later, Sterling taught me people can change and acknowledge past injustice. If so, then acting and speaking out is necessary and worthwhile, even when done by silent acts, even while acknowledging we should have done more.

From the dining room, Evelyn called us in to dinner. She carefully folded the last napkin and set it down beside a dinner plate, the napkin crisp and starched, the blue threads of its scalloped edges an echo of light blue flowers on the plate. Ice cubes cracked softly as they sank down in gleaming crystal glasses. Sterling pulled out my chair, and as I sat down, Evelyn lit the candles on the table. The flames flickered, caught and burned tall, the candlelight burnishing the sterling silver with streaks of soft gold.

"Gracious living," my mother would have said.

SEVEN
PLAYING AT RACISM

Elena Harap

Growing up in the South in the 1940s, a daughter of college-educated parents, I lived in a universe divided into Negro and White—divisions which shaped my experience of language and carried cultural judgments it has taken the rest of my life to understand and undo. In my White neighborhood in Nashville, Tennessee I heard little African-American speech, and what I did hear was often caricature. My friends and I played a game in which, in answer to any question, we were supposed to say, "Ol' Black Mammy's Greazy Toe" without laughing. White Appalachian Mountain language and lifestyle was also distorted and ridiculed, notably in one of our favorite comic strips, "Li'l Abner." We were taught to regard cultures other than that of the White middle class as inferior.

Rhymes I took for granted then come back with a shock now, for example, a word game that played on these lines:

> The poor old slave has gone to rest,
>   I know that he is free.

> His bones they lie, disturb them not,
> Way down in Tennessee.

My companions and I sang this in increasingly complicated forms, empty of meaning:

> The piggety-pack-poor old sliggety-slack-slave has giggety-gack-gone to riggety-rack-rest....

I made no connection between the song and the real-life Black people whom I encountered as a small child: Ludie Pearl Stott, brown-skinned, handsome and self-contained, who took care of me and my sisters; Julia Curry, a short, solid woman with burnished black skin, who did laundry and ironing; and a gray-brown silent man I remember only by the name of Hopwood, an occasional gardener. As a twelve-year-old, participating in an informal group called the World Interest Club, organized by a Fisk University professor's wife, I came to know Black girls of my own age and upbringing; meeting in our sponsor's home, across boundaries imposed by segregated schools, segregated neighborhoods, and racist legacy. We talked about world issues and cooked meals, trying out the styles of different countries; we didn't visit each other. While I realized that such a group was unusual for Nashville in those years, I had no concept of the brutal society that had given rise to our separation. The ways of slavery were not examined in American history class or my home.

Fifty years later my mother, at ninety-one, revealed her own childhood language of prejudice when she happened to hear the word pork in a conversation and recited:

> "Take a piece of pork, put it on a fork, give it to a Jew boy, Jew, Jew, Jew."

This from the woman whose shipboard romance with a "Jew boy"— —my father, Henry Harap— — lasted a lifetime. My daughter, hearing this, reminded me of a game she and her friends played on the front steps of our house in Boston in the 1970s:

> Chinese school has just begun,
> > No more laughing, no more fun,
> > If you show your teeth or tongue
> > You will pay a penalty.

"Chinese School" in turn triggered the recollection of a childhood counting song, "One little, two little, three little Indians." We would count to ten, after which the numbers were reversed: "Ten little, nine little, eight little Indians..." Not only were Indians seen as objects; they were made to disappear. The genocidal nineteenth-century fantasy of winning the West lived on in this banal, frightening ditty.

Perhaps each culture teaches its own stereotypes through children's games, and there is always the unknown "other" whom the children are permitted to mock and use as they please. We each begin in innocence and have to take in, then somehow transcend, the cultural lies stored in our inheritance of language.

Playing at Racism was originally part of a longer essay, "Words as Magical Incantations," in the anthology *Laughing in the Kitchen,* Streetfeet Press, 1998. It was also broadcast as a commentary on NPR.

EIGHT
CHERRY

Ken Williams

At eighteen years old, we aren't old enough to make life and death decisions. I'm thinking that I'm not ready for this as my stomach lurches on a nausea-producing roller coaster ride. The chopper I'm riding skims tall trees, hugs mountain ridges, and plunges with hurricane force down into the menacing valley below. Coursing low over a heavily armed enemy, we're low-flying bait.

The jungle floor is lush, a fusion of deep greens painted with velvet brush strokes, till it's not. Splotches of land have been torn up, burnt black, trees splintered into kindling as if a giant had rampaged through the land. The giant was one of the B-52 Stratofortresses, originally designed to carry nuclear weapons for Cold War-era deterrence missions, now these modern-day monsters carry five hundred to two-thousand-pound bombs, thousands of them at a time, to desecrate land and lives.

I'm new at this. I've only been in The Republic of Vietnam two weeks. And I'm scared, more frightened than I have ever been in my life. We are flying into the Valley of Death: the A Shau Valley into the meat grinder known as Operation Dewey Canyon.

The stories, the macabre rumors have fed our nightmares—by "our" I mean the new guys. They call us cherries. Most of the others on this resupply chopper, a CH-47 helicopter are battled-hardened Marines returning from either R&R or brief reprieves aboard hospital ships. A guy with a severe tic to his left eye brushed me with the haunted look they call the, "thousand-yard stare." Another guy's face is covered with scabs which he continues to pick at till they run with blood. Nobody talks. We're all trapped within our own foreboding thoughts. But one guy catches my eye. He smiles awkwardly. He too is a cherry. You can tell by his newly-minted green uniform that holds its color. He can't be much older than me. The uniform of the other grunts are tattered and sun bleached. Rags held together by perspiration, bug juice, and fear. They too must be my age, but they look so old! How did they get so old so fast? I briefly return the cherry's smile and quickly look away. I don't want others seeing me sharing emotions with the other new guy. I don't want to be tagged, guilt by association.

The chopper dives, and just when I think we will crash onto a rugged mountaintop it pulls up and lands hard. I expect my teeth to be shattered from the force, but they are intact. Before I can move, the battle-hardened grunts are up and out leaving the two new guys in the rear, following.

Within second' shouts of "incoming" ring out. A ghostly apparition, a gunny sergeant that I swear is Death pushes me and others into a slit trench burrowed into the ground. Then the mortars hit. The ground shutters. The earth groans. Dirt falls onto me in the dark, cramped casket-sized enclosure. I make my first vow of the day. Never again will I be caught underground during an enemy barrage. I would rather die on the surface than live in a casket.

The barrage ends. We crawl out into the light. Replacements, veterans and cherries alike are rationed out to depleted squads of the

Walking Dead, the Ninth Marines. That night more mortars rain down. But they pale next to what lies ahead. Me and the other cherry are put in the same bomb crater. He whimpers. He pleads. He asks God not to die. Tells me he will put a bullet in his leg; he'll do anything to get out of Vietnam. He becomes increasingly agitated by the sound of mortars, then the feel of the earth shuddering with their impacts. Then quiet. The more I offer him comforting words, the more my own agitated soul calms. It is the first of many traits I picked up in the war that will stay with me a lifetime.

Wearily we part the next morning. My new friend will, in fact, keep his promise and put a bullet in his leg a few months later.

The next morning we run into an ambush. Nothing big for the evening news, a couple killed. A couple wounded. Names to be etched on black granite wall years later. Forgotten statistics. Except, it's everything for us: The dead. The wounded. Survivors.

The following morning, predawn: from darkness enemy rifle fire and machine gun bullets light blackness. Worse yet: Friendly artillery fire falls short, blown into the bottom of the bomb crater. Steel shreds of shrapnel and jagged pieces of trees fall like rain. Stunned. Ears ringing. Sight washed out. Everything is a brilliant white. Wait for the ringing to stop. Hearing to return. Images of war form as vision returns. Still ahead that day a maelstrom of napalm and a firestorm of steel shards blitz the air. Carefully nuanced enemy mortars on our trail. Finally a sprint for life, then near-death by enemy machine-gun fire. A wounded Marine and I struggle to reach one of the last choppers out of the Valley of Death.

A lifetime of nightmares is born. And a troubling question that continues to haunt me: What happened to my new friend? Surely, they couldn't court-martial him. They weren't enough jail cells to hold all who mutilated themselves to get out of that hellhole. Dishonorable discharge? Guilt? Lies told to friends and relatives about his war stories? His wound. The only thing I know is that neither I nor anyone else can judge him. We all paid a price. We all carried a burden. Some of us fulfilled our duty, but honor became elusive in that moral quagmire. We were all too young. The previous day was my nineteenth birthday. On both sides, boys killed boys. And if we didn't die, we would have to live with that.

NINE
YESTERDAY'S HOME

Karen Ackland

My parents recently moved from the house where they'd lived for over fifty years, the house where I'd grown up, to a retirement community, near one of my sisters. They were both eighty-eight years old and both reluctant. Such a move had been in question for years, although my mother had made it clear that she loved her house and intended to stay. A lingering case of bronchitis weakened her resolve, and within a month, they'd put their house on the market and scheduled a mover. And I, who'd been eager to leave when I was twenty, felt suddenly kicked out of home.

A week before the move, I visited the Santa Cruz Museum of Art and History to see a multimedia installation by Ian Everard, a painter and interdisciplinary artist. In the exhibit, Everard had reproduced elements of his studio as a way to document a recent visit to his childhood home in Cornwall, England. There was a drafting table with a magnifying lamp, a director's chair, and an unfinished painting on an easel. To the right of the table was a five-drawer metal flat file. I pulled open the top drawer and heard Everard's recorded voice reciting the nursery rhyme, "*As I was going to St. Ives, I met a man with seven wives...*"

The drawer had photos of the town, a map, and a program from the cultural center. The materials weren't tacked down, but could be rearranged by the viewer. Subsequent drawers were devoted to the members of Ian's family: Dad, Mum, Ian, his brother. Many of the artifacts were common in each drawer; other objects were unique to the individual. As I opened the drawers the nursery rhyme was repeated, although slightly altered after the common first line: *As I was going to St. Ives, I met my Dad in former lives...* Or, in the bottom drawer, the one for his brother: *As I was going to St Ives, I emailed my brother several times ... So many questions about St. Ives.*

Well, I had questions, too. Why were my parents moving, and why was I so upset? I felt as petulant as a teenager—and as misunderstood.

I tried to imagine the contents of a similar file cabinet for my family: father, mother, three daughters. The common elements—the house, schools, church, pets—would be arranged with different priorities. We would have private as well as shared memories.

My parents had worked with the contractor to build the house. They'd raised three daughters, entertained friends, and planned to live there for the rest of their lives. For my sisters and me, it was the place where we got up every morning and went to school. We played outside with friends during the hot, dull summers and baked Toll House cookies in the kitchen on winter weekends. At night we dreamt of who we'd become once we left home, dreams that included houses of our own.

As I imagined a flat file displaying our family memories, I realized that despite our common history, my sisters and I had each inherited a different subset of our parents' values. When I was twenty, I'd been eager to leave: the house felt too conservative, my parents too protective. As the oldest, I'd inherited my father's value of independence and the importance of "standing on my own two feet."

Cindy, the middle daughter and the only one of us with children—inherited their belief in the importance of family and my mother's insistence on a tidy house. My parents had questioned whether they should move into a community near their friends or move closer to family. They'd consulted their minister who'd reminded them gently that their friends were dying and at their age, family was a safer bet. They were moving near Cindy.

Sue, the youngest daughter, acquired my father's hearty enthusiasm and my mother's concern for security. Possibly, my desire for independence and Cindy's focus on her immediate family created a vacuum that Sue felt the need to fill. She tried to protect our parents, long before they needed protecting, bringing brochures of retirement communities when she visited and calling the police when the phone went unanswered for a day. When I questioned her actions, hinting that our father had been embarrassed to find three police cars pull up in front of the house one morning as he was taking out the trash, she asserted that we needed to be responsible.

And I, the one who valued independence, insisted we needed to be respectful.

Only Cindy's drawer, the middle one, was the one we could all agree on, the one we communicated through.

The backyard of my parents' house faced onto a gully that adjoined the Angeles National Forest. When I was a girl, I played in the gully, although it had been years since I climbed down that hill. Some nights, especially when the dry season continued late into the fall, we could hear coyotes yip as they'd traveled down the canyon looking for water. This may make the area sound more rural than it was. Ours was a middle-class, suburban lifestyle—albeit a hilly one without sidewalks or sewers.

When I consider how I would arrange my file cabinet drawer, I think of the foothills, of the flat-yellow light that is characteristic of the Los Angeles Basin, of tree-high camellias and craggy live oaks, of craftsman architecture, the Pasadena arroyo, and the warm Santa Ana winds that sweep down the canyons in the fall. There are camellias and live oaks in Northern California where I live now, but it's the combination of the hills and the yellow light, the camellias and the oaks, that says home to me.

The duplex my parents were moving into was less than half the size of their house and objects that had survived a lifetime of usage and several major earthquakes needed to be sorted through and discarded. About a month before the move, my mother and I began pulling things out of the china hutch in the living room.

"Mother, why don't you sit down?" I asked. "I'll put things on the table and you can decide what you want."

But she couldn't sit still. "Look how dusty it is back there. Let me get a rag."

"I can do it." I ached for her as she decided what to give away.

She pointed to a tarnished platter. "I'll go start a sink of soapy water. Then we can get the silver polish out."

"Why don't you wait until you know what you're going to keep?"

There were glass platters and silver candlesticks that had been wedding presents, the good china and silver used only on special occasions and then washed by hand and carefully put away. When I was a girl, I assumed I'd have similar things when I grew up. But my tastes have changed, and I have no need for crystal platters or silver tea sets and certainly no place to store them.

Finally, mother said, "I'll just keep the everyday dishes for when we don't go to the dining hall. Everything in here needs to go." She got up and went into the other room. I put everything back in the hutch.

Later that afternoon, I emailed my sisters, nephew, and nieces, asking who wanted what. I felt like an auctioneer, answering questions and emailing photos. Going, going, gone. Although much too much remained. The following weekend my brother-in-law, bless him, said we couldn't throw away things that belonged to family and boxed up the rest to take with him.

Both my parents were raised in Los Angeles and moving to Bakersfield meant leaving an area they'd known all their lives. During the Depression, my father's father worked as a day-carpenter in Hollywood building movie sets. My mother's father patrolled their neighborhood during World War II, ensuring blackout curtains were in place against the possible threat of a Japanese invasion. Growing up they'd listened to the evangelist Sister Aimee Semple McPhearson on the radio and danced at the Coconut Grove. There were family stories about the house on 87th Street where my mother had lived and the bungalow on Harcourt Place where my father grew up. The house on Kingsley Drive that had belonged to my great-grandparents, the house they'd lost during the Depression, was mentioned with reverence. Curious, I once asked if we could visit. I'd checked a map and, although it wasn't an area where we normally went, it wasn't that far away either.

"But why would we go?" my father asked. "No one we know still lives there."

Cindy called the week before the move. "Did you know Mother threw away all the family photo albums?"

"What?"

"She said she won't have room for them where she's going. She took a few photos that she wanted and dumped everything else."

For my mother, tidiness has always trumped sentimentality, so I wasn't entirely surprised. Her bed is made before breakfast, appliances are put away after each use, and the newspaper is taken out to the recycling bin before noon. Still, it was hard not to feel like she was punishing us. As the mother, wasn't she supposed to be in charge of our memories? Wasn't she the one who knew which dark-haired baby it was in the photo?

"Could you save them?" Outside my window, goldfinches squabbled for a place at the bird feeder.

"The trash was picked up already. They're gone," Cindy said. "It's the last time I'll see the house. Before I left, I opened all the closets and said goodbye. Silly, huh?"

"No, I understand." I was grateful for her acknowledgment that this was our loss, too.

On moving day, I rose early and made coffee. The movers had packed everything the day before, and we'd spent the night in stripped down rooms. The furniture was still in place and clothes hung in the closets, but the cupboards were empty and taped boxes were stacked in the corners. Already the sense of home had been stripped away; it felt like we were squatters.

When my father came out to the kitchen, I asked if he'd moved his car out of the driveway so that the moving van could back in.

"Not right yet," he said politely, with the tone that warned he was tired of being told what to do.

When my mother appeared, I asked her if she had packed their medicine and a change of clothes, reminding her that the moving van would not arrive in Bakersfield for two days. "Not yet," she said. "I'm busy with some other things right now."

When I'd arrived three days earlier, I'd been reassured when my father outlined the move's timetable. By the next day, I was repeating the schedule to him. Since they'd announced the move, they repeatedly claimed that this was their decision. But on moving day, despite the unusual disarray throughout the house, the fact that they were moving seemed to have slipped their minds.

In the small bathroom off the back porch, my mother had filled the sink with warm water and ammonia and was soaking her hairbrush and my father's combs. Throughout my childhood, my mother periodically rounded up the family hairbrushes to soak in ammonia, so the activity wasn't unusual, just ill-timed. Her father had owned a business that bottled ammonia where my mother had worked during the summers—and perhaps that pungent order was a desperate, eleventh-hour cry to her own father for rescue.

My husband announced the moving van was on the way up the hill. He took my father's keys and moved the car. I led my mother back to the bedroom and helped her pack a suitcase.

That afternoon with the house almost empty, I found my parents on the couch in front of the fireplace. It has been pushed out of the way and was the only place left in the house to sit. My father was feeling light-headed, his face drained of color, and they were talking quietly while the rest of us stripped their house behind their backs. I'd come determined to help, but now I felt like a bill collector in some Dickensian novel, heartlessly throwing them out in the street.

My father watched as the movers picked up the pine hutch now wrapped in moving blankets and said, "Be careful with that. My father made it."

The movers were kind men; they knew they were dismantling a life. They were also on a schedule. One of them hesitated and then asked, "Was he Amish?"

My father considered this question before replying. "No. Baptist, I think." It was the church he'd attended as a boy eighty years before.

I took a photo of the moving van in front of the house and sent it to my sisters with the message, "almost done." I finished cleaning out the refrigerator, throwing away vegetables, the wheat germ my mother added to her breakfast smoothie each morning, and half-used jars of condiments. I washed the bins, swept the floors, and checked the cupboards and drawers. By the time we drove away an hour later, it was an empty house, dated and somewhat worn. I was tired from the long day, tired of patiently repeating myself, and anxious to get home and start cleaning out my own cupboards.

My parents have settled into their new place. Their two-bedroom duplex has been carefully decorated and looks like a scaled-down replica of their former home. The move was a good thing, but it was better for us than it was for them. Now when their answering machine has been mistakenly turned off, I call Cindy who drives over and turns it back on. She takes them to doctor appointments and does their grocery shopping. My parents delight in spending time with their great-grandchildren, playing school with the five-year-old and peek-a-boo with the baby. But, especially for my mother, some connection was severed when the moving van pulled away that day, some sense of who she is was lost. She resists going out and meeting her neighbors. She, who'd always been careful with her appearance, now wears the same pair of navy capris and black knee-high socks everywhere.

She's aware her memory is "not what it used to be," although when Cindy mentions the problem to her doctor, my mother rallies and passes the cognitive tests, except for the one about subtracting by seven. Her doctor writes, "Age-appropriate dementia" in her chart.

When I remind her that she can no longer drive, having failed the written part of the driving test, she pulls out her wallet. "I don't understand," she says, looking at the identification card that's clearly not a license. "Why did they send me this? Frankly, I'm a better driver than your father." She schedules an appointment at the DMV and then forgets to go. This happens multiple times.

One Sunday afternoon Cindy calls and, after assuring me that everyone is fine, says, "This morning when we got to church, Mom announced that she'd just stay in the car and work on her memory. She said the boxes in her mind had gotten messed up in the move and everything was out of place."

"Leave it to Mom to use a housekeeping image," I say. "Still, it's sad."

"We'll be there soon enough."

"That's sad, too."

If memories are the glue that hold the past and the present together, my parents' move weakened the adhesive bond. In the past, when I drove up the hill and parked in front of my parents' my father would have opened the door before I reached it. Later, as his hearing dimmed and gait slowed, he didn't always make it to the door, but always stood and headed toward me.

These days when I visit, I find my parents sitting in their armchairs, waiting. It's as if they've done this hard thing, a thing they didn't want to do, politely and without complaint, and now they'd like to go home. Of course, nothing excludes us from making the drive to see the house where we lived together. If we go, we should go soon —before the house is remodeled and changed past the point of recognition. But why would we go? No one we know lives there.

TEN
THE CEREMONY

Judy H. Reedy

At the age of forty-seven, I left a fairly comfortable job in Chicago for this one in Booniesville, Iowa. What a mistake. After my most recent promotion at the old job, I was losing insurance accounts and losing faith in my capabilities. I was overwhelmed and wanted a fresh start. The persistent negative self-talk never let up. "You're a fraud, Judy. You're not smart enough." I assumed a job in this country-bumpkin city surrounded by cornfields and cow manure would be more in tune to my skills. It wasn't. I expected the managers to be hick farmer-types that barely graduated from community college. They weren't.

I sat, waiting to be fired, with the conference room's harsh fluorescent lights shining on me like a spotlight. Kay and Nikki, The Terminators, sat across from me, their eyes staring above my head at the glass window overlooking the corridor. I imagined the reflection of my

Millennial and Generation X coworkers standing behind me watching the show and waving, just like the happy bystanders on New York's Times Square on Good Morning America. Today's afternoon amusement brought to them by the firing of the antique in the third cubicle.

As a mini bulldozer worked overtime in my gut, The Terminators, Kay (my manager) and Nikki (from HR), turned their gaze to me. I stared at, then picked at, my cuticles—waiting for this damn thing to start. There was a black file folder on the table between them. I grimaced with pain.

I felt underdressed for the occasion, my chubby body in twill khaki slacks and a white blouse. The Terminators were like twins, wearing their office uniform of dark Jones of New York-type designer suit jackets. I caught a whiff of rose, jasmine, and citrus from the fragrance, Chanel No. 5. So businesslike, these women, both with blonde short chin length "bob" haircuts and their "less is more" makeup.

"Sorry, but I *really* need to use the ladies room," I stammered. Kay accompanied me as I walked down the short dark hallway. She waited outside the ladies' room door like a member of the company swat team. There appeared Maddy, a voluptuous coworker –the only person on our floor who can get away with showing her cleavage. It always angered me that she could get by on her looks because her work ethic stunk. She batted her Bambi eyelashes while giving me a huge grin as we entered the restroom almost in unison. How strange that she'd be nice to me for once, on my last day. I sat on the toilet with my head in my hands, and my body trembling. I wished I could disappear down into the toilet bowl.

Back in the conference room, The Terminator's voices quivered as they took turns speaking. It pleased me that they sounded nervous after all they had put me through. "Two weeks' severance. We'll give you a box. Hand in keys...".

Three months before the firing, and one month before my 50th birthday, a similar event occurred. I was called into an impromptu meeting by Kay. A different conference room overlooking the street, but the same set-up. Jan and Nikki from HR and Kay on one side of the table, me on the other. Lots of throat clearing, paper shuffling, and eyes looking over my head at the window that looked out to the office cubicles. Before I sat down, I thought possibly I was getting kudos for something, or maybe even a raise. Not exactly. Out of the blue, ninety days probation for a series of unbelievable offenses: Condescending? Rude? Unhelpful? Complaints from clients? *Me?*

Flabbergasted, I looked to my left and over my shoulder as if to make the joke "who in the hell are you talking to?" I caught a glimpse of Pat, one of the male VPs, whose title should have been DEA— Division Executive Asshole. A six and a half foot tall and fairly wide monster of a guy, his presence in a room made conversations come to a halt with almost an unspoken requirement to bow. With reddish conservatively cut hair, beady blue eyes and a fake smile, he was Kay's direct boss. There he was, lurking right outside the conference room.

Most of my office communications were via email. A small percentage were by phone. I did - and do - have significant hearing impairment, but thought I did fine on the phone despite my handicap. Unfortunately, I inherited the gene for faulty auricular nerves and have a passion for eardrum busting Beatles and Rolling Stones music.

The ninety days between the probation meeting and the termination dragged on for what felt like years. The mini bulldozer paid my stomach a visit all day, every day. I would jump if anyone called my name from behind. The one good thing I remember about the ninety days is - it was the only time in my life when I lost weight without trying. The bad thing I remember is - I was buying Chardonnay by the case.

Because I made a fuss against the outlandish allegations, the soon-to-be Terminators appeased me and protected their employer asses by pretending my eventual firing wasn't already a done deal. They decided to have Tom, a kindly independent contractor liaison monitor my phone calls so that he could document all my rude chit-chat. He would give me a brief report when we passed in the hallway. "I think you sound fine. You're great on the phone. I really don't know what they are talking about. Keep your chin up."

During the ninety-day probation period, the DEA, Pat, seemed to ignore me. I went out of my way to avoid him because I had an unexplainable feeling he was responsible for my situation. I requested a transfer to a different department, so that I'd be reporting to a different group of people. I was turned down flat. The reason - I was on probation in another department. What a Catch-22.

"Judy, we are sorry to tell you that we are terminating you," Kay said. She continued, telling me that my phone conversations were fine during the probationary period. But, the fact that I asked for a transfer because of Pat, didn't sit well with the company. I couldn't think of anything to say other than "You're kidding." After the termination details were sorted out, I was escorted back to my desk to get my belongings. The entire floor was warned in advance and vacated. The room that usually had the sound of thirty employees pecking away at their keyboards or talking on the phone within their tiny padded jail cells... I mean cubicles... - was deserted.

Really? Did they think I'd pull a Smith & Wesson pistol out of my drawer, or, hysterically sob and throw things - like my wooden plaques of past achievements, framed educational certificates or photos of my kitties Cali and Ginger? As tempting as those options were, and since I didn't own a gun, all I really wanted to do was scram.

I wasn't ready for a very early retirement at the age of fifty. Not only didn't I have ducks, but if I did, they certainly wouldn't have been in a row. I *did* have a sorry excuse for a contingency plan. After the probation meeting, I bought into a stupid franchise and learned to make Candy Bouquets and Gift Baskets. I would become a creative entrepreneur and develop it into a huge enterprise and show their stuffy asses. Screw insurance and this place. Screw The Terminators. Screw Pat, and screw corporate America.

What made this so difficult was, back at my Chicago insurance job, at least for the first 15 years, I was a star performer. Extra office projects, continuing education, and overtime hours impressed my manager and the owner. I was the despised 'goody two shoes kiss-butt' positive person who caused the slackers to talk behind my back. I worked so hard because my career was my life. I had a husband, but no children to tend to after work hours.

Star performers like me (and for most of my career, I *had* been a star) breeze through continuing education when it isn't required. We lug work home most evenings and often go into the office on weekends. Accreditations, plaques, and framed certificates as evidence of our long hours line our office walls. Although I was able to accomplish a lot of work, my desk was always a mess. There was always a white lie on my resume' about having excellent organizational skills. Nope, these I did not have, but "clutter-bug' doesn't look good on a resume.

As a member of the Termination team waited outside the revolving front door downstairs, I retrieved my car for the last time from my spot on the rooftop parking lot. I inhaled the lingering foul odor of poured cement as I drove down the ramp, feeling nauseated and dizzy. I handed over the parking tag and keys and drove away in a daze. Trying to think of the positives, I pictured sleeping late tomorrow, the unemployment compensation I would collect, and the Candy Bouquet Empire I was going to build.

Despite feeling liberated from having to report to assholes, I was mad, and I wanted vengeance. I filed a complaint with the EEOC, Equal Employment Opportunity Commission, based on age discrimination and my disability of hearing impairment. With my caseworker snottily saying, "it may be unfair, but it wasn't illegal,"I lost. Despite losing, I found satisfaction in knowing I put everyone through a ton of work to fight my case. The olive-green folder, which was sent to me by the EEOC upon completion of the case, had six inches of paperwork in it, all describing how I suck. I couldn't bear to read the words, but I know that's what it said.

"Judy, you've *got* to get past this. Don't let this define who you are, or ruin the great career you had," my supportive friends and husband would say. I knew they were right, but being a good, if not a star, insurance professional was who I *used* to be. I was no longer that person, and it stung.

The candy bouquet and gift basket businesses weren't meeting their expenses. I added party dip mixes with funny names to my repertoire and sold them at local farmers' markets, craft shows and online. It was fun, but I could feel my brain shriveling up from lack of use, unless you'd call designing dip-mix labels and brochures challenging.

One sunny and pleasant Saturday morning about five years after the termination, as I was selling my dip mixes at a Farmers' Market, Sharon, an ex-coworker who sat across from me in the office, came into my booth. We spent a minute gossiping about the old days as she sampled the dips. I jokingly confided, "I never truly recovered from my termination, despite how fabulous this Dip Mix empire may look."

Her jaw dropped as her eyes widened. "You don't know why you were let go?" I shook my head and looked at her with a blank expression. Sharon went on to say that Maddy wanted to get back at me after I told Kay about problems I found with her work while she was on vacation. She was having an affair with Pat for a couple of years and told him she wanted me GONE. He made a case against me to get me fired. Sharon finished with, "The affair became public soon after you left, and Maddy was forced to leave."

I had a strong desire to kiss Sharon and then take out a newspaper ad or do a public service announcement on the radio. "I don't suck after all!" This knowledge should have given me the ability to move on. But, despite books such as: *The Self Esteem Workbook, The Gifts of Imperfection, Think Confident - Be Confident, Revolution from Within,* and *You Can Heal Your Life,* as well as a good shrink, I still remain negatively obsessed. I wallow in the disbelief that another human being could make fraudulent accusations, and back up those accusations with untruthful evidence—just to be assured of getting some nookie.

This wasn't *just* about losing a job for me, it was about losing *me*. Without children or grandchildren or a successful career, I am left with a black hole where a happy life should be. My career was my identity. My brain tells me I shouldn't continue to give my ex-coworkers the power of ruining my life, but my heart still aches. So, like I do with all my problems, I distract myself with Chardonnay.

Last winter, with the encouragement of my new shrink, I had an indoor bonfire of the contents of the EEOC folder. I prepared a new agey, positive-energy type of speech that The Dalai Lama would be proud of. All the members of my little family were present for the ceremony. As I read this important document aloud my husband nodded off, one cat licked her paw, and the other cat licked her own butt. After removing the paper clips and crumbling up wads of paper in my hands, I tearfully fed the clumps under the fireplace grate and threw some over the logs to ignite. I ended the ceremony with words of releasing it all and wishing them all well. I wish I meant it.

ELEVEN
CAUGHT

Lois Roelofs

I have Esther's shoes, the new white Skechers she'd packed carefully in her "wear home from the hospital" bag.

We did not expect my sister's death. We were ecstatic when we heard her surgery for esophageal cancer was successful. We were relieved when she transferred out of ICU, then greatly worried on her return. And we were shocked when she passed away twenty-seven days after surgery...from *complications*.

She'd called me the Saturday after her Monday surgery. She knew I'd be home with the flu and told me, "Take it easy and don't get pneumonia."

I said, "I already have pneumonia."

In her older-sister-by-five-year voice, she chided me: "Lois, what have I told you, over and over. Listen up. Take care of yourself."

The last few years we lived in Chicago, she came from Michigan to visit me for three days every summer. I'd take the 151 bus from Michigan and Washington by our condo to meet her at Union Station. She'd always introduce me to her Amtrak seat-mate, a new friend. Each year, I planned our agenda from the time she arrived (out for breakfast first) until the afternoon on the third day when I escorted her back by bus to Union Station. She insisted, as our final ritual, that she treat me for lunch at the Walnut Room in Macy's on State: their famous chicken pot pie, followed by their yummy, *calorie-free*, Frango Mint pie.

She didn't want to know what I'd planned, just what clothes she needed to take along. She liked surprises. Every summer, I picked out breakfast restaurants that had become her favorites (Lou Mitchell's, Toni's, the Yolk, and Pittsfield Cafe), and included plays at the Goodman and Apollo theaters, concerts by the Grant Park and Chicago Symphony orchestras, and lectures at the Art Institute.

And we walked, always logging in at least ten thousand steps on our pedometers. Every year, she'd say, "I want to walk your life. I want to be able to picture you when I get back home." With a chuckle, she'd add, "And, you know, I have to report back to my friends at workout. They want to hear about what my 'crazy Chicago sister' planned for me."

So, one year, we started from our condo at Randolph and Michigan and walked south to the museums (1200 south). I pointed out my favorite hangouts—Caribou to write, Starbucks for skinny decaf mochas, and the member lounge of the Art Institute to watch people.

We backtracked north to Water Tower Place (800 north). Along the way, I took her down an escalator in the office building on Pioneer Square, by the Chicago River, to the lower level of the University of Chicago's Gleacher Center where I took classes. "You are nuts, Lois," she said, "I don't get why you have to take so many classes." We stopped to stare in the windows of upscale shops. "I'd never feel comfortable going in there," she said. And I agreed. At the end of the walk north, I took her into my church, Fourth Presbyterian, and showed her the new modern addition, miraculously complementing the original Gothic architecture. She was mostly wordless here, stilled by its vast size as compared to her small-town church.

On the way back, at the halfway point, we veered east on Grand to Navy Pier (600 east). I pointed out Whole Foods that we called "whole paycheck," the AMC theater where I met my friends for our monthly movie date, and the hall of Tiffany stained glass inside Navy Pier.

Esther made it clear, for all this walking, that her feet liked her tennis shoes best. And that's what is not right about this. I now have her new Skechers that I know she would have worn during her planned trip this summer to visit me at my new home in Sioux Falls. I'd already told her there's not as much city walking here, but lots of nice nature trails, and that I'd started a list of things I wanted her to see: Phillips Avenue, the two-block main street lined with trendy shops and restaurants; 8th and Railroad, another trendy strip of shopping and eating places, the wooded nature trail starting just north of my home, and, of course, Falls Park, the tumbling waterfalls over centuries-old quartzite rock after which the city was named.

She thought she may be ready to come in June, but for sure by August. Instead, we buried her on April 13.

I'm home from the funeral now, over six-hundred miles away, feeling this big void. I miss her on our daily emails. During chemo and radiation; "First, I need to tell you I had a wonderful day!" Planning her post-op trip to Sioux Falls; "Let's just see how things are going. I'd love to come but also want to feel able to do things like we did in Chicago." Just before surgery: "Hi to many family and friends: This is general information regarding my upcoming surgery which is scheduled for March 13..."

I'll miss her spontaneous phone calls: "Lois, this is Esther. Glad I caught you home. Got a minute?" An hour later, we'd hang up.

I'll miss her yearly visits: "Let's do calendars. I need to plan ahead."

And I'll miss the fun we had every two years going to the Calvin

College Faith & Writing Festival in Michigan, splitting up the sessions we attended and filling each other in at night, over our drive-through for Wendy's chicken salads, in our beds at a Comfort Inn.

I may do a memorial walk—go to the places on the list I've started—wearing her shoes. I will tell her how much I miss her. She will laugh and say, "For Pete's sake, Lois. I lived to 80."

Three months have passed since we buried my sister Esther. I don't know how I'm supposed to deal with her death. Reading about grief hasn't helped. Emoting privately only takes the edge off. Talking with my one remaining sibling, my older sister Rose, raises more questions: What did we miss? How could we have been caught so unaware? Why didn't we say our goodbye's "just in case"?

Reviewing Esther's emails since her diagnosis, I find just one clue to help me deal with her loss. On the night before surgery, she wrote she was at peace. I know she was trusting her Lord and the doctors.

I guess since she was at peace, I should be too, yet I'm not. As a nurse, I wish I would have asked more, read more, remembered the seriousness of her surgery from my med-surg days over forty years ago. I'm angry at myself for not being more assertive, but then Rose reminds me that Esther wrote us that if we wanted to know more about her diagnosis to Google it. Which I did, of course, but now I'm not satisfied that I read enough.

I want to talk to her one more time. After all, even though my four siblings had lived across the United States, we'd always been in contact by a round robin letter and later by email. We'd shared everything from funky stories to favorite books to the feats and fiascos of our fifteen children and umpteen grandchildren. And, more recently, the ups and downs of aging—our falls and fractures, doctor visits and vital signs, lab work, x-rays, CT scans, and MRIs. So, now, the absence of Esther's daily input smacks me across my forehead every time I turn on my phone or open my computer and realize I won't be able to talk to her again.

You'd think I could handle her loss better. She's my third sibling of four who has passed away, in addition to three in-laws. My head knows, for sure, that death comes with aging. And I profess Christian beliefs—all those good things we say: *She's in a better place. It's a blessing she didn't have to suffer. We hope to see her again someday.* But these words don't help.

I can't stay caught in this anguish forever. Eventually, I want to be able to "turn it around," as my daughter gently tells her young kids who cry when they're out to play, and their feelings get hurt. But the ache of loss is not something we learned in school...like we didn't learn how to choose a mate, how to be single, divorced, married, widowed, or how to be a parent. And yet somehow most of us have survived whatever life presented, so with that logic, I know I will be able to look forward.

But I ask myself: *What can I do right now at the three-month mark of Esther's death to assuage my feelings of loss while also preparing myself for more losses in the future?*

I looked for clues in Esther's illness story. She didn't want to call me and our sister Rose with her cancer news. So, she'd emailed our daughters and asked them to deliver the news in person. I'd just left my daughter from a gray November morning of running errands and was sitting comfortably in my padded leather recliner eating a tossed salad when I sensed a presence at my front door. I could see her trying to peer through the semi-sheer white curtain on the side window. I raced to open the door, saw her tears and reddened face, and thought, *Oh no. Something's happened to her husband or kids.* She burst into the foyer, waving a white sheet of paper. "Aunt Esther's got cancer." And that's how the story of my sister Esther's cancer started for me, in my daughter's arms sobbing.

And then, too soon, the story ended with the final phone call from her son telling me that his mom was now in heaven with his dad and with Grandpa and Grandma. He added all the other members of my family who have died. He said I'd hear funeral plans by the next day, and I hung up and sobbed again, this time in my husband's arms.

My first thought when I remembered Esther's visitation and funeral were the dozens of younger people there, all identifying themselves as her friends. Some were from her workout group, others she had mentored in a young moms' group, while others had volunteered to drive her to chemo and radiation. And I realized most of my new friends are near my age, and I want to have some friends who are more likely to outlive me, so I should seek out younger pals. And, to my surprise, I thought, *I already have such a group.* A gal who I met in a class I took last spring invited me to her weekly coffee group. All those women are at least ten to fifteen years younger. I've gone a few times, wondering if I wanted to dedicate a morning a week to them; now I think I'd like to know them better. Their issues are those that I dealt with ten or more years ago: remodeling homes, planning children's weddings, filling their time in new retirements. Their stories energize me in a different way from those of older people like myself that tend to start out with health and move to traveling plans and back to the politics of health care.

My second thought took me to Esther's home after the funeral. Her daughter walked Rose and me through her two floors, telling us we could have whatever we wanted. We both saw several items of clothing that we'd given her. She'd always been grateful; she'd worn one of Rose's suits to her husband's funeral the year before. She said she'd tell her friends when another box came from her sisters. She'd go through it with her daughter and decide what each of them wanted, then she'd tell us, "I'll take the rest to missions."

On that tour, my last time in Esther's beige brick home on a corner, I took three things: a watch, a hat, and the Skechers, and, as I pondered what these could mean to me now, I realized that their presence could support me as I walk through my grief.

I wear the Fossil watch—silver in color with a fuchsia band that feels like rubber and looks braided. Wearing her watch will nudge me to remember that I still have a future of my own.

The hat, a pink Angora fedora-style she wore to chemo after her hair fell out, stands regally on a shelf in my closet. I see it every time I walk into our adjacent bathroom. When I look at it, I think of how Esther role modeled courage for all of us as she lost her husband and dealt with cancer in one year's time.

And then there's the shoes, the white Skechers. They sit prominently alongside my own tennis shoes on the floor in my closet. Every time I wear them, they will remind of her intentions to visit me as soon as she was well. To keep up her annual tradition.

I will wear Esther's Skechers and start the walk, as I'd planned, on Phillips Avenue, the two-block-long heart of my new downtown. As I walk, I will pretend our conversation. I will tell her how angry I am that she left me without warning, without saying goodbye. That her death caught me by surprise. And I know I will see her smile and hear her say, "Get off it, Lois. You knew the doctors told me the surgery may give me only five more years. So, we'd have to say farewell at some time or another. Possibly, soon."

I will remind her, though, our mother lived to ninety-five, and she will poo poo me and say, "Mother probably had better genes because she didn't get cancer."

Then it will be my turn to say, "I guess you're right. And I'll see you when my time comes."

I'll take her into the colorful Zandbroz Variety store at 209 S. Phillips to see the old ice cream counter. We'll reminisce about Uncle Bill's ice cream store in Long Island, New York, where we lived as kids and bought coffee ice cream cones for a nickel. I'll take her into boutique stores that are too fashion-forward for her taste. I'll take her for lunch at Minerva's, the historic woodsy-like restaurant at 301 S. Phillips that serves the best salads. We'll order the summer spinach salad with strawberries, candied walnuts, and goat cheese, much like our favorite salad at Arnie's restaurant near her home in Michigan.

And I'll see her eyes tearing up like they always did at Union Station when we had to part, and she'd say, "Oh, Lois, you are always so good to me." She'll add, "But this is enough for today. You know, I just had surgery. We can tour more tomorrow. Let's go back to your house and hang out. I want to hear every detail about your new life here. I want to walk with you.

A portion of this essay "Caught" was previously published on April 23, 2017, as "A Tribute to My Sister Esther – 1937-2017" on the blog lois-roelofs.com.

TWELVE
CODEPENDENCE, ANXIETY AND A SMACK ON THE HEAD

Patricia Byrne

When you have a loved one who is finally in long-term recovery, things begin to ease up. It's a slow process, but if you work on letting go and understanding you have no control, you inch closer and closer to being able to breathe. One day you realize you fell asleep and woke up without that band of anxiety gripping your chest. When your phone rings, and it's your loved one, panic is no longer your instinctive reaction. The fear stays with you, but you learn to keep it at bay. You remind yourself it's their life, and that projecting will do you no good. Live for today, be joyful for everything that is good in your life. Amen.

That's what I would have written a few months ago. But all it took was my mother's intuition—honed to pinpoint precision through years of codependency—to sound a warning bell, and I took ten giant steps backward. My son did not relapse, but he was having a difficult time. I could feel it coming, and the panic, helplessness, terror, and anxiety stampeded back into my life and, like puzzle pieces, settled into the familiar spaces in my brain shaped just for them.

We all have things that knock us down, make us want to throw the covers over our head and just hide out for a bit—preferably with some Ben & Jerry's to keep us company. I get that. But with my son in recovery, every bump in his road has concerned me. For some reason, this one really wound me up. Perhaps it had to do with the upcoming holidays. November and December can be anxiety-inducing in so many ways. We are expected to be happy whether we want to be or not, whether we are capable of doing so or not. All I know is I became anxious about my son's well-being. Not in a 'oh my God he may go out and use' way, but I was concerned because he was in a funk and having a hard time. What does a concerned mother do? She picks up the phone. And when my son had not answered or returned my calls in days – which, in all honesty, is perfectly normal for him, I mean, he's 30 years old for goodness sake, and I was already in a codependent anxious snit because I had a feeling; I opened the gates and allowed in the stampede.

I was really frustrated with myself. I understand about boundaries, codependency and how his life is his own. So why was I back here again projecting horrible scenarios in my mind? Because of course, I went from being concerned he seemed a bit depressed to picturing him in his room not breathing. That's a puzzle piece in my mind that I guess will take longer than I realized to banish – if that is even possible.

I was once again back to feeling anxious and helpless and increasingly frustrated with myself because I knew better. It's not my life, not my choices, and out of my control. Over the past six months, I had heard so many stories from all over the country of loss and relapse. We are fighting every day to get people to understand that they have to stop thinking, 'not my kid, it can't happen to me'.... I can't pretend 'that can't happen to me' when I speak to parents, spouses and loved ones all the time who have lost someone to overdose, and many of them to overdose because of relapse. My anxiety was at a level it had not been at in over a year, and I was adding to it by being upset that I was anxious. Still, I thought I had things under control.

... and a Smack on the Head

About a week before Christmas I had a very ungracious stumble as I was walking into a building. I had an appointment with people I had never met, parents of a friend. I could see them waiting for me in the lobby of the building, so as I pitched forward and the stairs came to meet my face, all I could think about was how mortified I was that they were witnessing my fall. As the crack of my forehead hitting the stairs rang in my head, I was simply grateful there were people there to help me. In the ensuing minutes, my friend's mother literally took the shirt off of her back so I could wipe the blood from my eyes and apply pressure to my head. The rest is really a blur, but there were so many people who helped me that day, from my friend's mother giving me her shirt, someone calling 911, and the paramedics and EMT's taking such good care of me. My friend went above and beyond, missing her daughter's school Christmas party to come to the hospital and keep me company as they stitched my forehead.

We all fall many times in our lives, though maybe not as literally as my klutzy trip up the stairs. We need to let go of the instinctive mortification we feel when we are caught being imperfect. Shame keeps us from asking for help. Shame often keeps us from admitting we fell. In my case I was embarrassed, but those around me leapt to their feet to help me. People with substance use issues have such a deep sense of shame when they find themselves having fallen that they don't want to ask for help. And often, the response is not people leaping to their feet. I have heard of SO many people who have rushed their loved one to the ER assuming they will find help for this life-threatening condition only to be told they can't do anything for them, here's a list of phone numbers....

The judgment and stigma and 'they did this to themselves' attitude makes those battling substance use too ashamed to ask for help, and when they do ask for help, it is not easily available. Wasn't I at fault when I fell? After all, I should have been paying more attention to the threshold of the building than looking around for the people I was meeting. Nobody told me I should have been watching where I was going. I got a lovely ambulance ride to the hospital and was brought straight back to be stitched up.

Two days after my fall the pain in my forehead became secondary to the headaches, dizziness, vertigo, nausea, and fuzziness of the concussion. My face was beautifully decorated for Christmas as the black eyes blossomed and the bruises formed tear like lines down my face. My forehead healed quickly, and the bruises faded, but it took longer for my brain to begin to function normally. I couldn't help but draw a parallel to those in recovery. Their bodies are cleansed of toxins, they gain weight and look like themselves again, but their brains are still healing. Functioning with a constant headache, reaching in frustration for words that wouldn't come to me, unable to think my way through a simple problem, and being totally overwhelmed walking grocery store aisles, I began to appreciate how those in early recovery feel. Overwhelmed, dizzy and trying to think through things that others think are so simple, all the while fending off cravings and PAWS* symptoms.

After the stairs jumped up and smacked me in the head, I didn't have time to be codependent and anxious about my son. I was too busy just getting through the day. Kind of like our loved ones as they navigate their way through early recovery. They don't have the bandwidth to worry about our codependence issues.

A funny thing happened when I stopped perseverating on my son's bout of blues. Nothing. Nothing happened. He is fine. Because whether I worry about him or not, he will do with his life as he chooses. He is choosing to survive. He is choosing to put one foot in front of the other. He is choosing to know that things don't get better overnight. It's still a slog 23+ months later, but he listens at his meetings, and others tell him it does get better. And he believes them. It does not make every day a walk in the garden, and some days are still 'I wish I could hide under the covers' days, but as he moves forward, there are fewer days where he actually stays hiding but instead makes himself come out to see the sunshine.

I had someone ask me during my weeks of anxiety, "but isn't your son in recovery and working?" Well, that just made me feel worse. Of course, every day that my son is in recovery is a good day, I am grateful and thankful and relieved, and I know that I should not project or borrow trouble. But here is the cold, bald truth. I know no matter how long my son is in recovery I will be waiting for the other shoe to drop. Some days that shoe will be way up high in the sky, just a pinpoint if you squint and look for it—but it's up there somewhere. Other times I will be living in the shadow of the shoe as it hovers inches above my head–because I don't have control. THAT is the reality. So I am done beating myself up when others think that I should be great and fantastic all the time because my son is in recovery. We all have our Ben & Jerry's as well as our 'wander the rose garden and smell the beautiful blooms' kind of days. Sometimes good things can even pile up on the same day.

My husband says, "you have to learn to be comfortable with being uncomfortable."

Maybe I needed that smack in the head to help hammer his words into my brain. The angry line on my forehead will fade, but it will always be a reminder to me that every day in life is not comfortable, and I'm just going to have to be OK with that.

*see Addiction is a Family Affair. We All Need Recovery at stopthesilencespeakthetruth.wordpress.com.

'Codependence, Anxiety and a Smack on the Head' was originally published in 2016 on StopTheSilenceSpeakTheTruth.com

THIRTEEN
TAKE THAT, DOORMAT

Colette O'Connor

"You're a doormat," says Kristin, the hypnotherapist. I perch, pathetic, on the edge of her soft, green sofa. The sofa sags from the weight of the woe I and countless hypnotherapies before me have brought to Kristin's office for healing.

"You're afraid to say the word no," she continues. I sigh. She's so right. *You're too nice,* the boyfriends pronounce at breakup. *You have the Disease to Please,* a segment of *Oprah* diagnoses. So, says Kristin before I slump further and forever into the sofa cushions in an effort to disappear my meek, unassertive self into a mote of insignificance. "I have a great idea for you." Sigh. Oh, woe. Whatever. "What would you think about a class in self-defense?"

Why I let Kristin convince me to join six other diseased-to-please women in a course the community Parks and Rec department titles Self Defense for Women, a class it presents as "the means to increase your personal safety at home, work, school and on the street," I don't know. Yet days later here I am, introducing my no-phobic self to

Tanya, our self-defense instructor. Tattoos color nearly every pore of her twiggy arms. Her will o' wisp legs and hips–what hips?–wear teensy, tight jeans. Five-foot-zero, Tanya tips the scale at maybe 93. She is so slight, in fact, it must be the 12 piercings of each ear, holes weighted with assorted, dangling...what are they, bear traps? tiger snares?...that keep her from being carried off on the breeze. If fierceness has a sister it, ain't she. But still, the tiger snares do seem ominous.

"Hi," she says, friendly enough. "So you want to learn to use your strengths against a perpetrator's weaknesses?" *I have no strengths,* I think. *I'm a doormat.* My friends in personal safety training don't look to have many strengths either. "Vanessa" sits wide-eyed on the group's fringe, shy. "Renee" focuses on her stiletto-heeled shoe when we are introduced. The lips of "Angelica" do move when asked for her name, but the silence that comes out causes Tanya to say it twice: "I'm sorry, what was that? Please speak up." The others look soft, pleasant, polite. *Nice girls.* That's what we are. I nervously twist my necklace of pearls and consider Tanya's tattoos. Kung-Fu fighters, are they? Fire-hurling dragons?

She says: "Do you want to end annoying behavior, harassment or physical threat?" *To be a doormat first, you have to lie down.* In my head, I hear Kristin's voice. It would be good in life if I could just stay standing, good not to let the world see the *Welcome* of me, coming and going. "Well," Tanya pronounces. "This is it, the class that addresses assertiveness, body language, the power of voice and," she does a chop-chop-flip thing with her hands, "how to do a lot of damage."

Vanessa looks stricken. Renee raises her hand. "Will we learn how to go for the, you know, *privates?*" she asks.

"We'll get to that."

Who knew that what we *get to* will be lessons in self-defense techniques like a "snap kick" that will shatter a kneecap. A "nose strike" that in a split-second can leave one broken and bloody. This is serious stuff, Tanya tells us; maneuvers proven effective at fighting off, God forbid, a sexual or other assault, as well as attitudes that tell friends, family, society, *Just you try*. However empowering this self-defense arsenal may be, however, here we people-pleasers are, paired up to practice an "eye-strike" that can send an attacker's eyeballs to the netherworld of agony. We are to press our thumbs into our partner's eyebrows to approximate the technique. Yet despite Tanya's instruction of "Harder! Harder!" the maneuver isn't exactly going over.

"Oops, I'm sorry," apologizes Angelica, as her thumbs poke me in the cheeks by mistake.

"Oh! Excuse me!" says Vanessa, who accidentally de-arranges Renee's hair in her eye-strike attempt; it's a fallen-over pouf she pokes to arrange back.

Tanya has seen our type. I imagine her Kung-Fu fighters are wizened to the fact nice girls like us need a chop-thing-*plus* to break through a lifetime of habit. All our years of *oh, no, after you!* All our decades of *please, never mind me*! Here they are, baked into cream puffs of women like me – I who end nearly every sentence with a question? You know, of self-doubt?

She tightens the screws of our training.

"OK. Now I want you to add the yell," she says. I cringe. Nice girls don't *like* to yell. "What sort of yell might you use in a potential situation? Anyone?"

"Um," says Angelica, "stop it?" Her voice is a flutter. If it were a color, it would be pretty peach.

"Good."

"No?" Renee suggests, tentative.

"Yes."

I offer an idea: "HELP!!!!"

"No," says Tanya, flatly. "That's victim-talk. Where there's victim-talk, there's victim-thought. Remember," she flexes her bicep and its Kung-Fu fighter grimaces with menace, "YOU'VE GOT

THE POWER." Tanya may be tiny, but her voice grows big, bold, *bad*.

Oh, right. I've got the power. *You let people walk all over you.* There's Kristin's voice again. I *so* do not have any power whatsoever. But Tanya insists that while in "ground defense position" – we're on our backs with hands crossed over our hearts and legs bent and prepped to kick – we run through the maneuver guaranteed to throw off an attacker even if our arms are pinned. In there is a pelvic thrust of a sort that causes Vanessa to take exception.

"Ew," she says. "I can't do that."

You *can*, Tanya says. The tiger snares clank a threat. "You have no *idea* how strong you are and powerful you become when your yell is added. Now, let me hear it. NO!" she booms. I swear the classroom windows rattle. We diseased-to-pleasers in unison flinch at the force of it. From that bitty thing! I stand in awe.

"No!" ventures Renee. It's the "no" of a mom denying her child permission to watch TV. Firm, but trimmed in sugar and spice and everything fairly nice.

"Louder!" urges Tanya, "NO!"

"No!" we nice girls give it a go. "NO!"

"LOUDER!" yells Tanya. "LOUDER!! Like this: NO! NO! NO!"

Yikes! I don't know how the windows hold it together.

"No! No! No!" Like the others, I try, "No!" Over and over and over. I'm on about my 12th when suddenly, something snaps: "NO!!!!" I roar. This is a no, unlike any no I have ever known. It is primal. Raw. *Dangerous*. It comes from I know not where. The others stare at me, stunned.

"Nice!" says Tanya. "Nice." I sense her Kung-Fu fighters' approval. Now, she says, let's put it together. Try "Stop it!" with a nose-strike. Or "Leave me alone!" with a snap-kick. Or how about "Go away!" with a good instep-stomp. Whatever you do, I want to hear it!"

So all we doormats do. STOP IT! GO AWAY! NO! As we roar

and as we boom, the nose-strikes fly, the kicks and thrusts and means of damage happen. I get the hang. I feel almost dragon-esque, hurling fire. "ENOUGH!" I flame and give the blue training pad a vicious kick to the kneecap.

"About the groin." Tanya's voice interrupts. She is moving on. We stop, breathless, for what surely is the class denouement.

"Here it is." She demonstrates by holding one hand above the other; we're to imagine the "area of vulnerability" dangling. "Slap, grab, twist, pull. You got that? Slap, grab, twist, pull."

No one wants to be the first to laugh. But there goes Renee – ha! – so the rest of us erupt; we snicker and hoot and slap and grab; we twist and pull, at least pretend, until, by the gift of a technique that could literally save us in far more serious circumstances, we come to rescue ourselves. Tanya cheerleads *Nice! Nice! Nice!* as our snickers turn to booms and our hoots to yells and we fight off years of fears by mastering this and the other moves that power-up something within us that I, for one, had no clue existed. After the longest time we wind down and finally, amid huffs and puffs and buckets of sweat, stop.

I am completely spent yet, strangely, satisfied, my heart thumping with the exercise. Vanessa flushed beams. Angelina speaks: "Whoohoo!" If her voice could swagger it would. Goodness me, it's Angelina unleashed! "That was *fun!*"

"See?" says Tanya, "It is *fun* to feel self-assured and unafraid, to know you absolutely can handle a situation in ways you never thought." What's more, she adds, mastering the physical moves of self-protection imprints strength into muscle memory. Feel power in the body and a woman can better own her *other* power. The wimpy one. The welcome mat that wants to duck beneath cushions in shyness and shame.

So, says Kristin, my first appointment back. I perch, perky, on the edge of her soft, green sofa. "How'd it go?"

"Just great!" I say, completely woe-free. And like the woman who wears fine French lingerie beneath her office outfit feels sexy with her secret, I feel fierce with mine.

"It's going to be a lot easier to say no from now on, isn't it?" says Kristin.

"Absolutely," I reply, and the Kung-Fu fighter close to my heart gives a little wink and a chop-chop, I like to think. He's only a wash-off tattoo but still. He reminds me: I have the power.

FOURTEEN
CAN YOU SEE ME NOW?

Karin Schmidt

In 1988 I decided to hide. I'd learned the hard reality of being dispensable from my employer; when I was diagnosed with multiple sclerosis, they wanted to cut me out of the company health insurance plan. That was before the Americans with Disability Act, and from that, I fully grasped the value of staying hidden.

Before I quit that job, I did some research, and the literature was divided on the if, how, and when to disclose. There were clearly two schools of thought, and I decided since my condition was nearly invisible, with few obvious symptoms, I'd take a shot at non-disclosure.

Moving on to each new job created a dilemma until the ADA became law. Then, I was only required to disclose if I wanted accommodations. MS remissions can be complete, and mine were nearly so. There were days I even fooled myself that maybe there'd been a mistake. Still, I always worried I'd be blindsided by a sudden flare-up. Memories of those days in the hospital, confined to a wheelchair, were only too vivid. Once in remission, my flare-ups were minor and short.

I was fortunate to have good jobs that allowed me to take a sick day when symptoms arose. I could close my office door and rest my head on my desk for ten minutes. I'd arrive early at meetings to avoid notice if my pace was too slow and always checked the seating situation ahead of time.

Working in highly competitive environments, I didn't want anyone thinking I couldn't do the job. I spent many years working in a medical education setting; they above anyone should have been empathetic. And they might have been if I'd been more open. But I couldn't take the chance of being seen as inadequate. Better to hide.

Next were several supervisory and management positions best described as sedentary, desk jobs. I'm proud that I managed my working life after diagnosis, all twenty-five years of it, without disclosing. My initial goal to remain ambulatory, employable, and invisible had been achieved. Then came retirement.

I smoothly adjusted to a slower lifestyle and went on looking and feeling healthy. But then along came the deterioration so natural with the passage of time. In 2016, a serious MS attack resulted in permanent loss of balance and leg strength; the dreaded moment had arrived. It was like being outed, unmasked. After decades of maintaining my façade of near perfect health, I was suddenly visible.

I'd bought the cane long before I needed it and stored it in the back of my closet. I knew the day would come and I wanted to be ready. I prefer to call it a walking stick. That makes it seem like it's a fashion accessory. It's a pretty little thing, with a dark-colored paisley-like floral print and a wooden handle. It's clear that it wasn't purchased for seven bucks at the local pharmacy.

I was forced to draw on the thoughts that helped me when I was first diagnosed, remembering how lucky I'd felt. A chronic illness is better than a life-threatening one, I'd told myself. The whole diagnosis/recovery experience helped me appreciate everything about my life that did work.

There is no fighting a chronic illness. At least, not successfully. It needs nurturing. Care. This may sound silly, but I had to think of my disease almost as a friend. And taking care of it has been the strangest relationship I've ever been involved in. Then I realized I had another friend.

These days I love my cane. Well, not actually love, but I do appreciate that pretty little thing with the paisley-like floral print. What would I do without this indispensable helper? And there are some unexpected benefits.

Showing up with a cane does clear the way to your seat in a theater or restaurant. Strangers scurry to open doors, offer an arm or hover around to be sure I'm navigating okay. While attending a Broadway play in New York, I'd dropped my cane under the seats in this crowded theater. A stranger a few seats away jumped up and got down on his knees to get it for me. There are so many nice people the world.

And I'm happy to say thank you. Though most of the time, its thank you for asking but I'm okay. That's another challenging thing about MS. I have to do as much as I can, be as active as possible, but I walk that fine line between being active and not over-doing.

When I was forced to be visible, my cane became a symbol of my disability, a signal of my decline. It broadcast my limitations to the world; it's taken quite some time to become comfortable with no longer being hidden. It's only in looking back that I realized the emotional energy it took to maintain that false self.

My biggest relief was to leave behind the heavy burden of secrets. Today, I'm clear and straightforward about what I'm able to do. For example, a recent lunch with girlfriends included a garden walk. I'd checked ahead to be sure there were sitting areas along the route. I have a new appreciation for railings, automatic doors, and ramps.

I get lots of comments on my cane. When someone says how nice it is, I usually respond that if you have to have one, it ought to be nice.

My cane gives me a sense of safety, and I do more with it than I ever did without it.

I look back on my work life, satisfied that I made the right decision not disclosing my condition. But what a relief to no longer have to search out places to sit or make lame excuses for why I can't perform certain tasks. These days, my cane and I are as busy as I want to be. I'm better and stronger, having accepted my limitations. And it feels good.

FIFTEEN
MINUTES OF THE MEETING

Elena Harap

My surname—Harap—is not a common one. As with other immigrants, at Ellis Island, my father's parents adopted or were assigned their anglicized name, and began the complicated process of constructing an American identity to go with it. Were they happy to relinquish the guttural *Cha-rap'* of their native Galicia, the familiar inflection of the Yiddish *Moishe* and *Yechovid*, to become Moses and Yetta H*ar'rap* ? I am told that another branch of the family decided to anglicize the same name to *Karp*, a serviceable alternative, but I never met these relatives. If I did, I might find it difficult to believe we came from the same roots.

Names have the power to define. Perhaps, as the immigration officer christened my grandfather with his new name, Moses paused in a moment of relief. Maybe he felt liberated from a life under the threat of poverty and pogroms. Perhaps he laughed. Given the pressures that must have forced him to leave Europe, and the enormous tasks ahead, what else was there to do? In the one family photo portraying this couple, posed formally with their nine children, my grandparents' faces are opaque, serious; but when I am with their descendants, I feel surrounded by warmth and sociability. At times I feel deprived, never having met Moses and Yetta, as if their live presence would provide an important key, a birthright which I must claim some other way.

As a child, I took my name, language, and American nationality for granted. My parents appeared to me quintessentially mainstream and middle class. My mother shared her Protestant background with my sisters and me; on religion, my father was noncommittal. "I am an agnostic," he said. Because we lived in the South and most of the Harap relatives were in New York, Connecticut, or New Jersey I rarely saw them. In addition, those who were Orthodox disapproved of my father's marriage and kept their distance. Only in adulthood did I take serious note of the fact that all the Haraps I knew were related to me and that we had a history in Eastern Europe. In my forties and fifties, I began to glean bits of information: my grandparents came from a town called Zalozitz, now in Ukraine; my grandfather arrived in New York in 1900 and got a job as a stitcher in a garment factory. His wife soon followed, and they raised a family of five boys and four girls; Yetta died quite young, of Hodgkins' Disease; Moses died in 1937, the year I was born. Every small fact became a treasure, and I think I even derived some pleasure from the very scarcity of information, the uncommon name and mysteries of my origin. On the other hand, if it is possible to miss someone you've never met, I missed my grandparents. I found the company of Harap aunts, uncles, and cousins stimulating and peculiarly affirmative. They made me feel at home with myself. The staid, strictly Kosher parents of the photograph had somehow bestowed a legacy of openness and humor.

In the first few generations of an immigrant family, or perhaps of any family whose collective life has been threatened in some way, there seems to lie a deep sense of the value of simple survival. When I met my father's brothers and sisters, as a college student in my early twenties, I found they regarded me with a pleasure that I had done nothing to earn. They appeared to be delighted with me for existing. I think it was my first experience of tribal identity, which, while it didn't detract from my individual sense of self, gave me a grounding that has lasted ever since. For them, perhaps, our meeting was not only added proof of the family's survival but a way of healing the breach caused by my father's marriage outside his religion.

A cousin who had encouraged my curiosity about family history celebrated his fiftieth wedding anniversary in the year 2000 and invited me and my husband to attend. One hundred years had passed since the Ellis Island naming of my grandfather. At the anniversary party, along with the joking and funny stories of how this cousin, a Connecticut farm boy, fell in love with a city girl, his grandchildren told him and his wife how much they loved them. I wondered what it would have been like to know my own grandparents and how they would have looked upon such a gathering. Thirty-odd people were scattered across the flower-bordered backyard of a two-story house in the town of Norwich, Connecticut; someone was cooking chicken on a grill; license plates on the cars parked in the driveway read Maine, Vermont, Massachusetts, and one family had traveled from California; grandchildren, great-grandchildren, and great-great-grandchildren were greeting each other, some meeting for the first time.

A collection of brown and black loose-leaf notebooks was passed around. These were the minutes of an informal organization called Family Circle that for years had organized regular gatherings of the descendants of Moses and Yetta Harap. The practice eventually ended as older members died, the children spread all over the country, and there ceased to be a geographical center. I was too busy snapping pictures of newly discovered cousins and hearing their stories to look at the Family Circle notebooks until the party began to wind down. My husband checked his watch; it was time to leave. I had been promised a copy of the Minutes but paused for a look at the originals. The notebooks, plain three-ring binders, had been gathered into a canvas tote bag; I drew one out and opened it. Some reports were neatly typed; some were in longhand. The business had mostly to do with where the next meeting would be held, usually in New York or Connecticut, and who would organize it, illnesses, deaths, births, expected births, trips, and news of far-flung family members. But in all this welter of predictable gossip, what riveted me were the *names*. On every line of writing there were Haraps, Haraps with ordinary names like Michael and Barbara and Walter, Haraps I had never heard of, a community in which this name was completely unexceptional.

The sight of these minutes—"the 65th meeting...the 72nd meeting..." gave me an indescribable sense of fulfillment. No longer mysterious, no longer a Harap manqué, I had become minute, a complimentary detail, a brushstroke in an endless scroll, its beginning out of sight, unrolling deliberately before me at that moment. Could this be the meaning of pride, a sensation I thought had to do at best with politics or at worst with empty assertions of superiority? This sense of recognition was neither; it wasn't even particularly exciting. It was so undramatically comforting that I had to admit I must have longed, all this time, to feel ordinary. Moses and Yetta must have wanted it too, in more brutal circumstances.

I closed the books and drove back with my husband to join a circle of *his* family in another part of Connecticut. This tribe, unlike mine, had ample documentation of itself, some eleven generations to feel ordinary in America—scrapbooks, letters, a well-researched family tree, and biographies of a few famous ancestors—and this had always seemed to me a great treasure. Is it because I am a writer that I need documents? Now I had found my own, the Minutes of the meetings of a bunch of people I scarcely knew but to whom I felt a deep physical and spiritual connection. One of my sisters has told me she experienced this same feeling when she discovered a piece of writing from our mother's side of the family, in England. At Cambridge, she looked up our English grandfather, found a witty essay he had published in a student magazine, and knew herself personally connected to that locality, that time in history, that young man who married and brought his wife to America, but died when their children were still in their teens.

The the essence of our identity, which appears quite strong as human beings go about the tasks of everyday life and children succeed their parents—one generation after another—is really rather fragile if we require so many proofs and documents and repetitions of our names. For my own part, I'd like to have it settled, once and for all: this is who I am and where I stand. But the Minutes tell me something else; the ground on which I stand is strong but shifting. It is created from moment to moment, year to year. The president opens the meeting, officers are nominated, but the president forgets to call for a vote so the secretary, his sister-in-law, laughingly reminds him of Roberts Rules of Order. Old business, new business: the Circle decides where to meet next year.

I sit at a desk in my husband's family home in Cornwall, Connecticut telling you the story of my grandparents' names. Trivial, indestructible minutes.

SIXTEEN
I'M SORRY

Joanne Nelson

I'm sorry about the time I ate a sandwich in your hospice room while you were dying. A portabella mushroom concoction, juices dripped from roasted vegetables mixed with flavored mayonnaise down to the napkin in my lap. Even worse, I drank a thick caramelly coffee topped with whipped cream—after scrounging for the extra-wide straw deep in my Panera's bag. The noise of those rustling pleasures so loud against the other sounds in the room: a televised soccer match that my brother, Kurt, watched with the volume down low and the subdued rhythm of the oxygen machine with its unchanging inhales and exhales. Your harsh breathing had finally relaxed, and your heart could remember—for a little longer anyway—what it was supposed to do.

But here's the thing: I didn't know it was wrong to enjoy food with my mother so close to death. You didn't teach me that, and somehow, I missed the obvious—that this was a ham on white bread occasion, or maybe McDonald's if takeout was a must.

It wasn't until the nurse came to check your vitals and gave me a quick, odd look as I took a bite, that I understood. My chest tightened, and Kurt, his own sandwich in hand said, "I guess it's a weird time to be eating." The nurse, whose mother must have taught her well, said, "Not at all, and there's food in the kitchen if the day gets long." She put her hand to my mother's forehead and wrist, then moved her blanket aside. "Look at your mom's legs," she said and motioned us over. She pointed out the fading color, the blood pulling back, as all your bodily resources tended to your heart.

Food in the kitchen. That's what our family was about. You were the queen of your stove—a frying pan with meat browning, a pot of potatoes boiling, a saucepan simmering with canned vegetables. The sound of a lid bouncing against a boiling pot was a constant throughout my childhood. All of the food on the table at the same time and still hot. This is a thing I would tell you about if, instead of drinking my coffee and using the straw to get to the cream dotted with beads of caramel in the bottom of the cup, I had pulled a chair to your bed, held your hand, and told stories for the few minutes left to us. Strings of events timed to the mechanical inhalations of the artificial oxygen, celebrations you could take with you wherever you're going.

If only. If only I had enough stories for however many breaths you had remaining. But that would be a different girl, maybe the girl from the photographs I never brought to the nursing home. The staff told us that residents like touches from home, but your shelves remained empty. I purchased a chair for the room and brought clothes when the seasons changed, but the pictures in the albums on my closet shelf were all wrong. The frozen moments contained too much of your backstory: anxiety, depression, addictions. I wanted store-bought frames with their pretend families. I wanted to tell you they were us, to point out relatives we both would have liked better than Uncle John with his roaming hands, Cousin Delores with her big house, or even your own mother with her caustic need to control. I wanted to display stories of an alternate history, one I could share with your favorite nurse and the kind aides. It's the daughter from those photos, not me, that could have held your hand and waited to eat her sandwich somewhere else.

Instead, you spent those last hours alone in your small bed, doing the hard work of dying—your grown children in the same room, but not close. Your wrinkles fell away, and your mouth hung open and dry, except for when I swabbed your lips and tongue with water. My brother watched television while I took notes, already playing out how this sandwich thing would go, how it balanced against the rest of the long afternoon.

I wanted to do what good daughters might do before you passed— to protect myself from some future guilt or distress about this day. As the afternoon slouched on I moved closer, settled in a chair next to you and held your hand, and I did tell you things I remembered—the way we read together, those triple-layered, chocolate birthday cakes, how you folded your hands during the Hail Mary each night when I was little. You stood at the foot of my bed with your hands pressed together palms and fingers flat against each other, trying to set a good example. I tried to keep pace through the Our Father and the Hail Mary, stumbling over words I found difficult—blessed art thou amongst women—and lines I didn't understand—the fruit of thy womb. My own hands were a lazy fold, fingers woven together, no matter how many times you told me that looked sloppy.

I called your brother and had him talk to your unresponsive ear, let him make whatever peace he found necessary and say his goodbyes. The earlier crinkling of the Panera's bag and the empty coffee cup betrayed me though, revealed me. The loud noise and the pleasing food in the death room exposed the dissonance between my studied actions and who I really am, and I'm sorry for that. Sorry I didn't hold your hand earlier and say I'd miss you. Sorry I didn't feel worse.

When your heart stopped, Kurt and I were sitting beside you, touching you. We waited a long time for an inhale that wouldn't come. The oxygen machine continued though. Carried on its useless rhythm until we reached over to shut it off.

SEVENTEEN
SUFFERING MIGRAINES

Catherine Jones

When one travels as much as I do, and when one suffers as many migraines as I do, one develops a method to suffer in some comfort. My tactic is to find the nicest place around and lie down there until I can again see the world without a colorful, painful aura. If anyone has an objection to my presence, I just don't care. I can't care; I have to focus. I become assertive about taking care of myself when my general default is often one of deference. Not so when a migraine hits.

I had a mother who suffered headaches. Usually, she did not give me much space, but when I was in my darkened, silent bedroom, she allowed me to lie there.

As I ventured further afield from home, my suffering became encapsulated in more exotic surroundings. These headaches empowered me to claim my space.

While taking a cooking course in Florence, Italy, I became debilitated. I left the hot European-picturesque kitchen to lay on the cool tiles in the hallway. People from the class and those who lived in the villa had to keep stepping over me. The madam was quite bewildered until I held my head in my hands and moaned. She got the gest and gently pulled my hand until I figured out to stand up and follow her to a sparsely decorated room with antique furniture and walls painted with pastoral scenes. She directed me to large bed with a hand-embroidered bedspread, probably centuries old. I lay down as if on a cloud.

She left, but I could not find peace. The walls were sending off vibrations. I was restless, almost fearful. "Oh hell, not another psychic encounter with my surroundings." When my restlessness became overwhelming, I staggered back to the kitchen as the owner's son was regaling the standing members of the pasta-making class with stories of the villa's occupation by the Nazi commander in charge of Michelangelo's city during WWII. Sixty years later the evilness of the man was still clinging to the frescos in the bedroom where debauchery seemed to be lingering.

On another excursion, I found myself on an island in Western Samoa, Savaii. I had hitched on to the coattails of a large Samoan family going to a wedding in a very small, rather remote village. One evening our hoard decided to go to a restaurant. One second, I was fine, and the next I was seeing more light in the sky than just the stars. I collected ice cubes from other diners—dipping my hands in their glasses without permission. I wrapped them in a napkin and bathed my head until the ice melted and my napkin grew wet and tepid. I could no longer sit there. "I am going outside." I couldn't bear the lights of the restaurant. "I am going to sit on the beach."

I found an unoccupied fale, the old type Samoan house, an oval structure with posts to supporting a thatched roof. I crawled in. The moon was shining on the water which was a good omen as I have been given the Samoan name Sina, meaning moon. The sound of the waves lapping the sandy beach was soothing, the muscles in my body relaxed in the arms of the Polynesian night.

Fa'afatai, one of my traveling partners, wandered over. "Mom told me to come see if you are ok. You really need to leave the fale because it belongs to someone who we do not know."

I responded in the most authoritative voice I could muster, "I don't care." The owner never came, but the entire family migrated over to my shelter under the starry Samoan night.

Okay, I have also had migraines in some pretty awful locations. On a long train ride in China I, a Westerner on an expensive tour, was housed for the night in a sleeper with three others on the tour. The door to the compartment locked, I was contained in a bubble, but the bathroom at the end of the corridor was so putrid, peeing and throwing up in the stall was not an option. I lay on the top bunk willing all bodily fluids to stay put.

A knock on the cabin door was immediately followed by a man in a very official looking uniform bursting into the tiny space. As the official rapidly spoke, my eyes grew larger for I had no way of knowing what he was saying, but it didn't sound good. I was relieved to see the tour's Chinese guide come into view; he did not look relieved. I was not going to talk unless spoken to, and then very carefully, I told myself, for in my altered state the directions could not be too complex.

Our guide spoke, "The officials would like the person who is sick to come with them."

I replied, probably too quickly, "No one here is sick. The person must be in another car." I had no intention of following a Chinese official anywhere. I locked on my mother's eye, then my sister's, and then my niece's. No one spoke; they allowed me this decision, unusual for my family.

Our guide continued, "We are going to be passing into Hong Kong in a few hours. Ill people are not allowed through the checkpoint."

"We, in this compartment, are fine," I politely explained. And simultaneously I felt the immediate urge to vomit, which I did—timed to the screech of the train wheels. Fortunately, he did not look back.

As I lay on the bunk trying to sway with the rhythm of the train, I worried about the next customs checkpoint. I never did anything wrong with regards to customs, but apprehension weighed me down even further. What if I had picked up some strange disease that I would be bringing to the outside world? I finally fell into a sleep just refreshing enough for the stand-up-straight, and answer–easy-questions-coherently tasks of the next day. Of course, an American passport usually gets one through most international borders, and so it was with me.

Sometimes the world demanded my attention as when the small private school where I taught couldn't do without me. I called the vice-principal at 5AM, and at 7AM, he was on the phone saying he could not find a substitute. It was Friday; I wondered if all the other teachers who needed the day off were as sick as I. I guessed they had just planned better. I brushed my teeth, but no make-up. I put on underpants, but no bra and a muumuu for I wanted nothing touching my body. I got a brush through my hair, and that was good enough. I made an ice pack, put on sunglasses, and hoped if I threw up, it would be on the kid who gave me the most aggravation. For most of the day, I lay on the floor while sixteen special education students did their thing.

When my car broke down, I sat in a gas station for hours while the fumes lodged an assault on my brain. I did have to resort to using another unsavory toilet room. I looked the attendant in the eye and said, "Come on, if you can fix a BMW you can swish a brush around a toilet." He lowered his eyes.

However, let me recount a headache in a more picturesque environment, a hotel in the hills of Burma, which was once the private home of a rather important English officer. Myanmar, as the country is now called, had just opened up to travelers. When the announcement for the trip arrived in the mail, I was on the phone in seconds to reserve my space. The following Sunday, while at my son's house for dinner, I was devastated to learn my daughter-in-law was diagnosed with breast cancer on Wednesday. The following

Monday she would be entering the hospital for a radical mastectomy.

My son's wife, Dalia, was born in Cambodia as the Khmer Rouge marched into the capital city. She is from a family of intelligent, hard-working survivors, and she went into efficient mode, organizing family needs and medical priorities with efficiency. Their son, my grandson, is a charming 8 year old who has been categorized as borderline autistic, and Dalia kept his life as routine as possible despite the demands of treatment.

Dalia was still going through radiation and chemotherapy when the time for the trip arrived. Life was moving along somewhat normally, so I did not cancel my plans to see an Asian country that seemed frozen in time. I wanted to see this corner of the world before development would take its toll.

I was ahing and wowing my way through the country of pagodas while thinking about the changes life had delivered to my son. I thought about the three of them while washing an elephant in a river, riding in a hot air balloon, climbing the steep steps of a pagoda at sunset. At supper, with a group of fellow travelers, I asked if anyone knew where I could check my email. I wanted to check in on my daughter-in-law, worried about her response to chemo and radiation.

One of the women said, "I just sent one, so I'll show you where and how after dinner." She went on to tell me about her friend who died when her son was eight, the same age as my grandson."He's on Prozac and suicidal. In the future, you will thank me for telling you so you can be watching for mental issues."

Her words hit me like a sock in the stomach. I just looked at her with a glare, wanting to accuse her of thinking that she knew every-thing about everything. Instead, I got a migraine. The air draped me in too much moisture to allow sleeping. In the middle of the night, I put a sarong over my nightgown and wandered to the lobby looking for ice, instead found the cool night air on the veranda. I sat on the ground trying to yoga my headache into the recesses of my mind where it would lurk just below the surface. The next day I walked by the sitting room to view the viperous woman crying on the shoulder of the tour director. I didn't care about her problem. I was not going to be part of turning a trip to Burma into constant acrimony, but neither was I going to be friendly to the bitch.

The migraine found me again, and I retreated to my room. The housekeeper came in as I was retching in the bathroom. She knew no English, I knew no whatever-she-was -speaking, but she knew I needed help. She turned on the shower and helped me in. Then she helped me to the bed. She sat with me for a while. The world sent me her, and I was appreciative. She earned her big tip.

Migraines still slither to the surface. They engender me with an outward assertiveness that seems counterintuitive to weakness and pain I feel. This is not a time I am good at considering the needs of others. I might lie on the floor in the silent darkness for three days. I might be impolite or improper. And sometimes, even when I'm at my worst, someone will speak softly, show me a better place to rest, a better way to be, or sit with me until I can again navigate the world.

EIGHTEEN

ELECTING TO LOVE

Dawn Cogger

I wanted to pummel my husband, and did, with the side of my clenched fists pounding his bare chest in rage and fear, saying, "How could you vote for that bastard?" My partner voted against every value I hold. He stood tall and still in the clothes closet in bare feet and beige trousers, holding his bright green Costa-Rica t-shirt in his right hand; he looked down at me with a frown of total mystery and shocked eyes. We saw each other across a wide divide.

Hours earlier I sat beside my husband while he was at the computer. I said in a defeated tone, "Trump won." He turned his head toward me with a deadpan expression and said, "Yes."

I remember saying (while holding back my emotions), "It's scary, and it's a disaster." My husband said he hoped Trump would appoint some seasoned leaders like John McCain and Newt Gingrich. I told him I hoped he was right, but I thought he'll fire anyone who didn't agree with him. "He has no respect for anyone, even himself." I tried to be calm. My insides churned something foul. I wanted to scream, yell, cry, and run. I couldn't see how our country could elect or survive Trump.

I knew my husband was likely to vote for Trump before the November 2016 Presidential Election. I didn't want to believe it. It affected our conversations and spontaneity. I was on edge. On rare occasions I expressed my thoughts, again working to stay calm: "Are you aware Trump cruelly harassed the Muslim couple whose son died in Iraq in OUR military-they, in the ultimate pain of losing their son? Trump bullies. We cannot put up with bullying. We're trying to teach people not to bully, and the President is modeling bullying AND getting away with it. He labels all Mexicans as drug dealers and rapists. There's a tape I purposely didn't listen to of Trump talking about genital groping of women." How often could I bring this up without evoking defensiveness? Would anything persuade him? I couldn't be silent and still respect myself. These are Trump's conquests and our horrors I say to myself. How could it get anymore wretched? How can I live with my husband? Do I have to be nice about this? Will I destroy a marriage that I've cherished?

My husband worked for the U.S. Government in the Department of Defense of our nation for 30 years. He retired from the Air Force Reserves as a Lieutenant Colonel. He'd been a loyal Republican. Little did I know how loyal.

In a recent calm conversation with my husband, he said the government's purpose is defense, to defend our borders, and work on trade agreements. The rest, he said is done according to the individual. The government shouldn't be creating programs as though it knows what's best for everyone. Except for military personnel who have given to our nation, people need to work; no giving benefits to people who don't work. He said he's waiting for President Trump to change the number of years that people can be in Congress, prevent congressional leaders from lobbying, and change the rules, so congressional leaders don't receive more benefits, including healthcare, than our citizens. When I asked how he deals with what's happening, he responded, "I just let it go. I know they're going to do what they want to do. Our congress believes its job is to constantly focus on re-election."

I was born in Canada and came to the United States when I was eleven with my father and mother, my younger sister and younger brother. We came through the Immigration Office in Toronto, Ontario and were issued green cards. My father worked with Spruce Falls of Canada. He had a new job with the brother company, Kimberly Clark in Wisconsin. I went to high school in Neenah, WI, and when I applied to go to college at age seventeen, the US government required me to make a formal declaration I would become an American Citizen. After college, marrying, working, and pregnant with my first child, I pondered whether Canada and the United States would ever go to war and test my allegiance. I decided, likely not.

I was sworn in as a US Citizen with a diverse group of people in Minneapolis, MN. Weeks later I voted for Richard Nixon (a Republican) for President. His administration ended up in Watergate. I watched the trials.

I took citizenship seriously and felt privileged. My voting decisions are based on reading from a variety of sources. I sought out neutral news stations and listened for respect, honesty and facts about platforms and ideologies of candidates. I'm not a political party person, or haven't been in the past.

I was the first born in a family of three children with parents who expected children to be seen and not heard. You did as you were told, you did as you should, and you set a good example. I wasn't allowed an opinion or to speak up about anything. I was afraid of my mother with her venomous, seething, harsh words and shaking finger, or her complete silence for days without explanation. Both made me shrink.

Mom taught us manners and took us dressed up to the restaurant in Green Bay, WI that had a toy chest for my young brother to explore after behaving at lunch. On annual trips to Canada to see relatives, we had the special treat of riding on the streetcar and having rice pudding in downtown Toronto, Ontario, Canada. My mother gave me a love of music, playing the 35rpm records of The King and I, South Pacific, and My Fair Lady.

A few times I feared my father would hit me; however, I knew he loved me. He gave me my love of nature by taking me, at age nine on a five-mile hiking and fishing trip in northern Ontario. Just us. There were few words, but his actions spoke of appreciation as he held the tree branches that swung back as he briskly walked ahead of me for five miles in the dense forest. He cupped cold, rushing water in his hand from a sparkling stream to my thirsty mouth. He taught me to carry the fishing rods facing forward through the forest while looking for the rare pink Lady Slippers. He taught me how to paddle the canoe, dipping the paddle with effective quiet, so we didn't disturb nature.

Both parents provided our home, food, clothes and our educations. There was no verbal or physical display of affection from either parent.

My parents taught me to adopt their opinions and to act in accord with their expectations. A good woman is patient, obedient, and a good listener. I knew how to play nicely with others, and that I was important to my parents. They taught me how to make peace with authority and to meet cultural expectations. They taught me out of love and in the context of their experience—even though it left me powerless. What I didn't learn from them was: I had needs; I had a brain and opinions; I had a voice.

My husband grew up with three siblings. He was the oldest, and his parents expected about the same from him, work and "Hold up your end." When he was eighteen, he was to support himself entirely, which he did, getting his Master's Degree in Engineering. From fourth grade on, he had a paper route year-round, saving the money for his education. He didn't play sports, though wanted by a coach. Instead he worked and saved his money. He is a practical, math-gifted person who is usually flexible and patient. He loves classical music and world travel.

He tells me he loves me every day; sometimes I can't take it in, silently wearing my invisible six-foot, seven-inch high emotional barrier to match his physical presence.

During the six months prior to and after the election, my thoughts were often focused on my husband's much younger sister who was diagnosed with pancreatic cancer. Because my sister-in-law and I were friends and I was a retired nurse, we communicated often, and she spent two weeks with us to recover after her major surgery. She had been an independent, responsible, healthy person with four young adult children, had her own home and her own small brass business. Because of the disease and treatment, she couldn't keep the pace her life required though she desperately tried. She needed the Affordable Care Act (ACA or Obamacare) insurance.

During the C-Span hearings for the ACA when President Obama was new in office, I listened and learned who was involved, or not, in creating the policies and what was legislated. I was excited we would finally have healthcare insurance for everyone. Since then, I've spoken up when the topic of health insurance arises.

Since Trump was elected, I have written and called congressional representatives and senators. I've written snail-mail letters to members of Congress, too, both to those who oppose comprehensive health insurance for all and to those who work for it. I've had a letter to the editor published in *The Daily Advance* newspaper in Elizabeth City, North Carolina, (our home) which included telling readers some of my professional experiences: of working in hospitals, long-term care, a multi-specialty clinic and as an investigator of abuse and neglect in healthcare. In the editorial letter, I asked readers: What are your values? What makes you want to get up in the morning? I added—we are not self-sufficient; that's an illusion. In addition, I said, a friend of mine is sick, and due to the illness and treatment, she can't work. She needs the ACA insurance. Many others are sick and some are born with anomalies. These people need care. And in every other developed country in the world, they would get it.

I'm crushed that my husband didn't care enough to vote to preserve the ACA. He doesn't see he's voting to stop treatment for his own sister. How close does it need to get for him to consider that health care shouldn't be only for the lucky? I don't think we will ever understand each other. I'm so angry and helpless about his illogical stance. His sister didn't get pancreatic cancer to scam the system.

I was shocked with myself too. I've had a lot of grief in my life, but I've never expressed my loss and anger with a person in this physical way. I'd hit my husband. I won't be a victim and I shouldn't be a victimizer.

The decisions to speak out, to overcome my instinct to shut up and be nice, to act each day to fight for healthcare and political issues that bump up against my value system were made when I went on a weekend retreat the Friday after the Tuesday Presidential Election. The night after the election I couldn't sleep. I feared nuclear war with volatile leaders. I feared for my grandchildren.

Also, I knew I had to get away for solitude, to be with God to help me be the person I want to be. I want to walk in peace. That's been my mantra. I believe I must walk in peace to facilitate peace; however, it doesn't mean I don't take responsibility for injustice and act for justice.

My ill sister-in-law had been recovering with us in our Wisconsin home, about a week after her major surgery. She still needed lots of rest and frequent small meals, but she and my husband could make it without me, I decided. I thought they were better off without an angry me. I made the call and got the last room at Holy Wisdom Monastery, an Ecumenical Christian Monastery run by Benedictine women in Madison.

During the retreat I felt insane with the alternating tears and anger, the awakening in fear, realizing each time, Trump was in charge, that Trump would be interacting with the leader of North Korea—two volatile leaders. Trump was making decisions about health care, the environment, cabinet appointments. He was in charge, and I felt helpless.

AND my husband and I were not together in this. How could I live with him? It feels like sleeping with the enemy. How can I share my body and mind? What was this doing to my soul? How does he do it? It doesn't seem to bother him. I can't have sex and detach myself from it and not pay a price. We both pay a price. I refuse to sacrifice myself.

After the second retreat day with times walking, praying in silence and in shouting, journaling, sharing with others, and being in God's compassionate lap, I was able to review how I already live my life. What are my values and where do I give my time, talent, and money? Do I change or affirm those life-work decisions to support my little world, and our larger world?

I decided I would show love and appreciation for my husband when I sincerely could, while being gentle with myself, honoring my brain and body.

I would continue to support the International Crane Foundation to help the environment in preventing the predicted mass extinction of world species.

I would continue to educate myself and spouse when he seemed open. I'd listen to him. I'd study current administration's proposals for healthcare coverage and fight for comprehensive coverage with my vote and voice.

I would continue my participation with the Ecumenical Christian Retreat Group in North Carolina, and my membership in Spiritual Directors International, which fosters reaching across traditions, cultures, and religions to honor The Holy and all humanity—even within the challenge of working to honor a husband who loves me, yet voted for Trump. I can't make sense of this. I can choose to love without understanding, for better or for worse.

NINETEEN

SEEING THROUGH MOHAMMED'S EYES

Catherine Lanser

What were we thinking? I had waited for what seemed like my whole life to get married at 42 and now a few months later, speeding through the High Atlas, I was probably going to die.

My new husband and I had only been in Morocco a few days, but I was beginning to wonder if our families were right. Although they had been worried about radical Islam and the Ebola threat when they fretted about us choosing this locale for our post-nuptial getaway, I was sure it was the driving that would do us in. We thought we had taken the necessary precautions. But our family saw this "Middle Eastern" country as dangerous for other reasons. The fact that we were traveling to Africa during the height of Ebola crisis didn't help either.

"It's not even close to where Ebola is," we said.

"Isn't that a Muslim country?" they asked.

"Yes, but it is very safe," we said. "We are working with a tour company and will have our own driver."

We would discover that driving, with or without Mohammed,

would add a level of terror we had not planned on. My new husband and I had our first hint of what was to come as we left the magical and crazy maze of Marrakesh where there seemed to be no stop signs and where SUVs, cars, mopeds, motorized tricycles, bicycles, carts led by mules, and carriages led by horses, all competed in the same roundabout. We were glad to finally be on a straight two-lane road heading into the mountains even if our heads were pressed into the headrests in response to the uncomfortable acceleration.

We whizzed past pedestrians and motorbikes sometimes with two passengers, often carrying precarious cargo such as glass windows. When someone drove too slowly, Mohammed sped up within inches of their bumper, then jerked out to pass them. Sometimes there were too many cars in the right lane. In response, he stayed in the left lane so long it seemed he was playing chicken with oncoming cars before squeezing back in, just a few cars forward.

As we rose into the mountains Mohammed continued to drive as if we were on a schedule we didn't know about, passing cars both on straightaways and turns, as did other drivers. Seeing the fear in our eyes from the rearview mirror, he asked, "Is this okay?"

We nodded yes, not sure what would happen if we said no.

"I've been driving these roads for 16 years," he told us. "Is very safe."

I wanted to view the beautiful red mountains outside our window, but closed my eyes and grabbed my husband's hand instead. I tried to believe our driver, but the fact that we had nearly hit an oncoming tour bus while passing made me doubt his confidence. In Marrakesh, he had pulled over on the side of the road to take a cell phone call and apologized after, which I took to mean that he wouldn't be taking any other calls while driving.

But it seemed he was apologizing for pulling over because now in the mountain passes he not only took calls, answering an almost constant ringtone that whistled to get his attention, but also dialed the phone. Eventually, he took so many calls his earpiece gave out, which he tried, unsuccessfully, to fix while he drove. When he finally gave up, he used the handset to talk. When he wasn't fiddling with the phone, he gave hand signals to other drivers that we tried to decipher.

At our first stop, my husband and I stumbled out of the vehicle, thankful for the dusty, steady ground and caught our breath as women from a cooperative quietly sat on the floor using a hand mill to crush the seeds of the Argan tree. We could purchase the treasured oil to be used cosmetically or at the table. Afterward, we crossed the road to take pictures of the vista and the mountains we had just climbed, whispering to each other about the driving before Mohammed snuck up behind us. He offered to take a picture of us together with the landscape behind us.

I hoped he had not heard us speculating that he was hurrying us through the peaks so he could be off the clock earlier. As Mohammed finished his cigarette, we spoke out of earshot, sharing techniques on how to make the driving more palatable.

"I've been closing my eyes," I said.

"I've been hanging on to the door handle," Joel said.

In the coming days, we'd employ other techniques such as looking out across the horizon, looking down at our phones, or eating dried pineapple, when we felt nauseous.

But no matter; when we felt as if we'd found a solution, Mohammed or the environment upped the ante. The driving would get a little more daring, or something new would appear on the road that we'd never imagine such as a donkey or a group of children causing Mohammed to slam on the breaks or swerve to avoid. And yet, the evocative country kept calling. As much as I wanted to close my eyes, I wanted to see more of its sights and its people.

Once after a night camping out in the Sahara, where sound was absent save for the snorting camels, we were surprised again as Mohammed went completely off the road, cutting through a field of pink boulders. Our car banged through the field and rattled out all desert tranquility. On the other side and back on paved road, he parked the car and walked around it as if he were a rental car agent making sure the car had not sustained any damage or flat tires. Happy with what he found, he began driving without a word.

At night my husband and I would pile out of the car and wish Mohammed a good evening and say the little Arabic we knew, shokran, for the pleasure of the day's drive. I would stretch my toes out to ease the cramping caused by digging them into the floor mats all day. "See you tomorrow," we would say.

"Insha'Allah" he'd say, meaning *God willing*.

We'd laugh a bit at the irony of the greeting, thinking about how it seemed that God's will had been what we needed to get through the day. Our nights, on the other hand, were safe and comfortable. We were dropped off in the most remarkably remote places. One night it was a cool pool perched in an oasis of date palms, the ever-present mountains ringing us. Another evening we walked through a small farm. We'd discuss the day's drive, and hope for straight roads with no mountain passes the next day. But we knew it didn't matter where we travelled. Even as we passed through small villages our car didn't decelerate, the speed staying constant the whole time we drove.

As we walked through the farm, we watched cows grazing in the dusty earth among the pomegranate, date, olive and palm trees. We climbed into the tower of one of the beautiful red kasbahs on the property. It rose up out of the earth, its layered red dirt and stone walls carrying us up to a prime perch to see the sunset falling over the now blue mountains in the distance. As we breathed in the heat of our honeymoon, assuming we had found our perfect moment, a loud asthmatic wailing rang out below us. We noticed the donkey in the pen long after it noticed us, now running toward us, disturbing the stillness of the twilight.

It wasn't much different than Mohammed's incessant honking during the drive, although the horn sounded like Beaker on the Muppets to me. It was an odd accompaniment to the loudspeakers blaring the call to prayer of the muezzin from the mosques and a strange soundtrack to the men we glimpsed kneeling on prayer rugs in between buildings as we tore through their towns.

One day, again racing through the mountains, I steadied my eyes on the far-off dwellings built into the cliff. My head jerked as Mohammed did a U-turn across the road and onto a rocky path down into the valley between the mountains. We again seemed to be traversing on something that was barely a road, but this seemed more perilous, more like a path of erosion cut through the side of the mountain met by a wide-open chasm waiting for us below. We swayed like palms in the back seat as the SUV bounced down the mountainside.

"We will see the first Kasbah," he said, his eyes flashing in the rearview mirror.

If there were any time to close my eyes, this was it. I shut them tight while the Land Cruiser careened and plummeted, my stomach following suit, and didn't open them again until Mohammed began to speak again. We had arrived in a kind of reverse landscape; the brown mountains had turned into a green valley and cities of earthen mud buildings had replaced the peaks.

"Kasbah Telouet," he said, parking the car.

We walked closer to the kasbah, which a guide dressed in traditional Berber attire explained was home to T'hami el Glaoui, who had partnered with the French to remove the Sultan from power in 1953. The outside of the kasbah seemed to be a ruin of red soil as if it had been covered in earth and the dust had been wiped away to reveal a palace with glass, ironwork, and silky white stone beneath. Here and there full walls stood straight among clumps of land, and as we entered, we could make out what had once been a regal courtyard.

As we walked through the door, we absorbed the beauty hiding inside these earthen walls. There were tiled floors, mosaics, carved wooden doors, scrollwork around the windows, colorful faded silk panels adorning the ceilings, and elaborate Moorish archways leading from one room to the other. It was as if someone had built an intricate sandcastle, hiding all their treasures inside. I could see now why

Mohammed was in such a rush to show us this and the rest of his country. It was yet another veiled wonder along the road.

As we approached the car, I began to worry about our return trip back up the rocky path. The terror of the driving was bad enough, but more than that I wanted to travel with my eyes open, so I wouldn't miss anything. I was glad when we continued, that we did so through the valley, if still quickly along hills layered with shades of white. Mohammed used his hands to tell us about the salt harvest and pointed out the many colors streaming along the road. He likened it to the diversity of Morocco's religions and people, which he said many did not know included Muslim, Protestant, Berber, Catholic, and Jewish. He spoke with a pride that seemed somehow modest.

I saw it and relaxed into the velocity of moment, and into the seat next to my new husband. We had not been crazy to choose this place to start our journey as a married couple. The driving in Morocco been unexpected, but the landscape and the people had been so too. Mohammed's urgency had become a viewfinder. And there was so much more ahead of us. God willing.

TWENTY
LEMON AND LOVE ON CRETE

Julia Older

On the overnight ferry to the Port of Iraklion, I climbed to the deck in the gathering twilight, peered into the dark Aegean, and hoped to silence the voice which had pestered me since I toured Delphi: *"You have to climb the mountain to earn what you learn, and not choke the Muse to get it."*

The boat rocked forward and back, swaying and belching fumes out its stack, a *deus ex machina* moaning like Frankenstein.

While I was topside, the cabin had turned into a vomitorium, and I fled back into the open air. If there had been a mast, like Ulysses I would have tied myself to it—not only to escape the incessant Sirens luring me with their lyrics but to distance myself from my retching cabin mates.

Iraklion is what Italians call a *stella di mare,* not a big star but small and luminous. Across from my balcony overlooking the old port, I found a tantalizing restaurant. Not knowing Greek, how would I order? The irresistible smells of cloves and mint, seared lamb and fresh lemon, triggered dormant taste memories from student days at the University of Michigan.

The most popular dishes at the Cottage Inn in Ann Arbor were pepperoni pizza and roast beef on Wonder Bread with glue-like gravy. Waitressing paid minimum wages, and students rarely tipped. But there was one perk. After the noon rush, I sat at a booth in the back and could order anything on the menu. I'd seen the Greek owner George making soup from scratch and decided to chance it. He placed an overflowing bowl before me, disappeared into the kitchen, and returned with a saucer of sliced lemon.

"But George, I'm not having a Greek salad." "Put in soup," he ordered, handing me a slice. "In the bean soup?"

He flashed a winsome gap-toothed smile. "Put in."

George waited in his greasy grill apron. I squeezed the lemon into the smooth white bean soup, gave it a stir, and ate a spoonful. He nodded approval as I emptied the bowl.

Milton must have had waiters in mind when he wrote:*"They also serve who stand and wait."*

It was a small gift for George to serve his part-time waitress, but he left me with an indelible taste-print of Greek, lemon, and love.

Seduced by the smell of seared eggplant, I entered the Iraklion store-front restaurant. A floury-armed man in an apron hurried from the kitchen to my table. I tried Italian. He called for help. A young boy skipped out of the kitchen and gently touched my wrist. "Come."

The bull-leaping boys of Crete had slender bodies and round hips. So the Minotaur in the Labyrinth bellowed at them as well.

A deli case in back was filled with meats, cheeses, pastries. The boy bobbed down and emerged with a pita bread in his hand. He placed a finger at the corner of his olive-black eye, a gesture which in Italy meant "pay close attention," and pointed to a bowl of fresh mint, lettuce, and tomatoes. I nodded and tapped the glistening squares of feta cheese beside it. The simple pita sandwich he placed before me was the first in an array of homemade dishes proudly served and humbly eaten on that mysterious Greek island of Crete.

Entering any building from the bright island light was like standing at the entrance to a cave, and the Iraklion Museum turned dark as a movie theatre. I wound through the maze of rooms squinting at handwritten labels identifying a jumble of artifacts. Around a corner, I came face to face with three white Parian marble musicians looking for all the world like Cubist statuettes by Brancusi and Archipenko. I slowed and glanced at the label. No wonder the band was so polished. They'd been jamming in the Cyclades 5000 years.

> *The Art, the manners, the refined signs of a civilized race stay vitally yours, Cretans. There is no death.*

I'd rushed through several dimly lit rooms pursued by Crete's bare-breasted, snake-hurling fertility goddesses. The year before, my footloose husband traveled to Crete and brought me one of these molded plastic Minoan Barbie dolls as a gift.

> *Yet, in the squalor and filth*
>   *of the Eastern Iraklion marketplace, there is nothing remotely similar to ancient Greece.*

My parents-in-law desperately wanted an heir. During my husband's next Mediterranean research cruise, I stuffed the bust-popping epoxy goddess in a drawer and returned to my newest lover, Dante Alighieri.

The following day, on a short bus ride to the celebrated Minoan Palace at Knossos, the rocky coast of Iraklion fell away, supplanted by lush orange and banana groves. The transformation was so startling I thought either I'd fallen asleep or boarded the wrong bus. What a wondrously strange place Crete was turning out to be.

The similarity between the regal bearing Minoans of ancient Crete (3000-1100BC) and native Etruscans of Italy (c1200-300 BC) survives in their wall frescos. Both cultures were gay, though not frivolous, artistic yet not self-absorbed. Minoan bull leapers might be boys or girls. In Etruria, too, flute players and diviners could be either sex. Their incantation rang in my ear.

> When we were dancing your back arched
> and you looked
> wide-eyed from beneath the curve of your arm.

Plumbing was installed throughout the Knossos Palace, and while the Queen enjoyed a good soak in her bath, artists mixed paints and designed frescoes in their studio complex. The sun and stars flowed down light wells supported by palm-trunk pillars adorned with a colorful panoply of Minoan flora and fauna.

The Delphic Oracle whom I hadn't heard for a while—and, frankly, didn't miss— whispered: *"The soul joins the body on Crete. Do you hear me, G i u l i a ?"*

I looked around the red and gold throne room where King Minos presided. Far below this inner sanctum in a maze of tunnels and caves bellowed the King's prize Minotaur.

Wise Ariadne, with the foresight of Queen Pasifae foaming bestial images of the bull, burst like Venus from the sea.

Thesus, who was sent from Athens as a sacrifice to the half-man half-bull, fast-talked the King's lovesick daughter Ariadne into unwinding a ball of yarn (clew /Aka clue) so he could slay the monster and escape. Seeing no further use for her after they fled, he ditched her.

Hoping to circumvent the persistent Delphic voice harping on Ariadne's failed love—as well as my own—I rushed headlong through the Knossos Palace. But it was no use. At every turn the Oracle, which had stalked me since I'd met her at the Theatre on Mount Olympus, hounded me with her pithy presage: *"You have been through four of seven acts. Seven planets spun into your house in Act One."*

The Palace tour guide wandered off for a smoke. Another polyglot guide was telling tourists about a Greek poet. Full of leggy wonder, I trailed him into the Knossos Banquet Hall.

"The ancient Greek poet Simonides once was invited to a banquet to recite his poems," the guide was saying. "The banquet host offered him dinner instead of payment. Offended, Simonides headed down the palace steps, reached the road and turning, witnessed a devastating fire consuming the banquet hall and guests."

"Now that's poetic justice," I said.

He explained that angry relatives mobbed the hall demanding they be told who sat where, so they could collect the bodies. When the stunned host could not remember, Simonides ordered a parchment and drew a plan of every single person seated at the banquet.

"This is the Second Act. . . " the Oracle hissed, *". . .The Word Banquet. It is followed by The Cave Womb Of Your Mother. The Three Sisters play a leading role in Act Four."*

My younger sister survived my parents' acrimonious divorce and was planning a big wedding in which I had no part. My older sister married a writer she'd met at the University of Michigan. Photos of their first child arrived with his first book. But like everyone ever close to me, they grew so remote they virtually disappeared.

As I rode the bus back to Iraklion, I dismissed Botticelli's Three Graces smiling in eternal beauty and recalled a recent image of their ancient Greek predecessors, The *Caritas*. With luck, their charitable love imparted the healing source that would make me whole.

At Minoan moonrise, I was sitting in the storefront of the Iraklion restaurant again, eating the last bite of galaktoboureko (a custard-lemon dessert fit for Aphrodite) when a man walked in. Until that moment, I never really had seen a man.

Only the waking sun has ever stared at me that way—though once a man from Crete flew straight through my eyes, and landed in my heart.

We call women beautiful; men tall, dark and handsome. These are sadly inadequate words for the disappearance of truth and beauty. The man's high red leather boots and black shirt suited him to ride horseback. A woman, followed, not subserviently, but with a determined confidence that her man had business. To look too long into his face I knew was a transgression, and I stared down at my empty plate, turning my gaze only to follow him out.

My favorite enters the sacrificial center. Earth moves slowly, faster, charges. I watch the bull-leaper tense, grab the horned mountains and vault safely to the other side. My love is captive.

My love is alive.

That evening by coincidence while reading Henry Miller's *The Colossus of Maroussi*, I was startled to discover how closely his impressions resembled mine:

> *"From the countryside, the Cretans come into Heraklion garbed in handsome black raiment set off by elegant high boots. They are the most handsome noble males I have ever seen."*

A week later, I saw the man again, and others. A race unto themselves.

Minoan bulls leap with tall, muscular bearing and alert faces. The ancient sense of the word dis-crete derives from the ancient Cretan law: *"the right to remain silent."* He was such a man.

Note: Minoan of Knossos poem in italics by Sicilian poet Salvatore Quasimodo translated by the author. Non-italic poems by the author.

TWENTY-ONE

WHOM TO LOVE

Annette Van Veen Gippe

I knew I was taking a chance when I took Klaus, my adorable, friendly date, to my tenth high-school reunion.

Rather than arrive alone and embarrassed, I wanted my former classmates to see that I had "landed" a husband.

Folks not seen in 10 years flowed into the ballroom filled with screams of recognition and joy. Everyone talked of their successes since high school, and most sported their charming "original" spouse. I imagined that my decision to have him at my side helped me fit in.

He disappeared sometime during dinner; a common occurrence in our shaky year-old marriage—not surprising.

I learned in Al-Anon to detach from his alcoholic behavior. So, I proceeded to enjoy the evening and danced like 1965; did the Mashed Potato with Marion, the Swim with Steve, Twisted with Tom, and Boogalooed with Bobby. Then we all did the Loco-motion. It was fun: I was fun.

The evening ended too soon. Some friends asked me to join them for a nightcap at the top of the Hancock Building. When they inquired about my missing husband, I replied, "He'll find his way home...let's go."

As we walked past the empty coat room, I looked in and exclaimed, "There he is now!" Indeed I saw my "darling" husband on the floor, humping Ginger.

My shocked friends asked, "Is there anything we can do?" "No." I explained, "He will come home when she runs out of beer."

I attended my twenties alone reunion alone, and I fit-in very well.

Born to loving, kind and respectful parents, I looked forward to one day meeting my own perfect mate. My parents met on a blind date right after World War II in France and married 6 months later. Inseparable, they their predictable love seemed almost boring. I didn't know their love was extraordinary in its reliable warmth. One of their routines was to never go to bed angry. There were arguments, but father ended them by hugging my mother and patting her behind. Smiling parents welcomed me to the breakfast table. Whatever the dispute, they handled it respectfully and quietly. As I sit in my living room, focused on a large black and white photo of the beaming couple on their wedding day, I wonder where I went awry in my relationships.

I grew up in "no sex before marriage" years, yet matured during the sexual revolution. I justified my sexual encounters by believing that they would lead to marriage. Not so. But I kept on trying. Unfortunately, my husband-picker proved to be a bit flawed.

My loving parents believed the marriage to Klaus would not last five years. But, after seven years of meeting my less than stellar boyfriends, they decided to put on a good party at the South Shore Country Club on Lake Michigan. My handsome curly-haired man with beautiful blue eyes sparked with charisma as my father walked me down the aisle in the classic Gothic church. We proceeded to the country club. The room had floor to ceiling windows that looked out on the cloudless sunny day, bright green golf course and the lake. From start to finish, all I ever dreamt for my wedding day came true.

From what my parents told me, I can visualize their 1946 wedding day in Cannes, France. I picture them riding the Army motorcycle; an Army Air Corps officer, in uniform, with his bride, her veil blowing in the wind as they ride along the azure Mediterranean.

Our Hawaiian honeymoon started with champagne on the airplane, followed by sunny days on the beach and romantic nights in the suite. It ended when the house detective appeared at our door to see what all the screaming was about.

This began four years of living with an adorable but unreliable alcoholic and drug addict. We divorced. However, those shocking, hilarious and outrageous situations that shattered our marriage somehow still make me laugh.

I married "rebound man." Tall, handsome, and mustachioed, he did not drink and came directly home after work. A reliable man, he offered stability, or so I thought. However, he quit his job as soon as he received a letter from Publisher's Clearing House that said: "You might be a winner." I am not kidding. Not the most ambitious guy, he continued to look for easy money.

I ignored the warning, and we decided to start a family. However, after 18 months of disappointing fertility treatments and adoption attempts, I accepted that no one would ever call me Mom.

Communication dropped off, as did the sex. I'd jumped in too soon after my divorce. I had wanted to prove that I could have the successful "perfect" marriage my parents had and because he did not drink I thought our marriage had a great chance of success. I was wrong, and he was wrong.

We ended. I arrived home from work, and he announced, with no emotion, that he did not want to be married anymore and was leaving me. "Why?" I asked. His reply, "If you don't know, I'm not going to tell you."

Ten years later, I met Ron on a business trip to Colorado. He was tall, sexy and joyful. We carried on a long-distance relationship for well over a year enjoying telephone calls, flowers and long weekends together. The relationship flourished. Our time together was idyllic. He showed me the tranquil vistas of Colorado, and I introduced him to the bustling rhythms of Chicago. When he asked me to marry him, I told him that I could not have children and would not go through the painful process of adoption or fertility treatments again. "That doesn't matter," he declared, "I love you, and you are all I need to be happy."

I got pregnant on our honeymoon. At 40, I did not even suspect. Three months passed before I took the test. Positive! Shocked, but elated, when I told him, we danced around our living room. Our daughter Brittany arrived, and 18 months later, Emily Rose joined us. The wonderful father began disappearing; at first for hours, then for days. When he walked out, the girls were six and eight. On his way out the door, he said I had tricked him into marriage by telling him I could not have children. He has seen the girls less than ten times in the last 21 years.

My journey of love carries disappointment but not devastation. I can remember what I loved about my men. I am a mostly fearless survivor. My faith in God's grace helps. I am grateful for all my blessings…especially my strong, smart and beautiful daughters.

My prince never arrived as expected, well, at least, not yet. Maybe I should let my next prince pick me.

TWENTY-TWO

ONE TOO MANY GRAVES

Cheri Todd Molter

"Mommy, time to wake up," Megan says. She shakes my arm, unrelenting until I open my eyes.

"I'm up, honey. Thank you." I lower the foot of the gold velvet La-Z-Boy and stretch my cramped body. My back muscles scream in protest; I've been sleeping on this recliner for too many months. *It's Greg's turn to sleep out here. I'm sleeping in my bed tonight,* I think, noticing that the television is still on. I grab the remote, hit the power button before I stand up.

"You're welcome," Meg sings, picking up her plaid L.L. Bean backpack off the wood floor and placing it on the loveseat. "Have you seen my library book? I need to return it today." I watch her, head bent and brunette pig-tails swinging.

"Check the table. I saw it there yesterday." She walks to the kitchen, and I head to my bedroom to get dressed.

As I pass my son's bedroom door, I knock, then open the door a smidge. "Logan, thirty-five minutes before the bus; you up?" Silence. "Logan?! Time to get up, kiddo!" I walk in, open the brick-red curtain, light streams through the window, reflecting off of the pale gray walls. Then, I plop down on his bed, jostle him from side to side. Like me, he's not a morning person.

"Okay, okay...I'm awake." Logan groans in a sleep-laden voice, turning toward me. "Stop bouncing me around." He untangles himself from the gray wolf comforter he got last Christmas and reaches for his glasses as I leave his room.

In the hallway, I notice the door to my bedroom is shut. *Damn, does that mean Greg's still home?* I turn the doorknob, step inside. The bed's empty and unmade; there's no sound of running water from the master bath. *Good, he's left for work.* I take a deep, calming breath, pause to appreciate the morning light as it filters through the gossamer-thin ivory window curtains, illuminating the sky-blue walls. I do love light. I get underwear, jeans, and a shirt from my dresser, and go take a quick shower.

Afterward, I dress, twist my long, wet blonde hair up in a tortoise-shell clip, slip on a pair of Crocs, return to the kitchen where Logan's finishing a bowl of Cinnamon Toast Crunch while Meggie, next to him at the table, reviews her spelling words. Third grade has been more challenging, but she's still at the top of her class.

"Time to go, guys." I pick up my purse and walk towards the back door. They file like ducklings behind me. In the rear of the line, Logan locks the door with his key—a new privilege and responsibility since he's thirteen—and hops in the front seat of my navy Buick, folding his long legs in around his backpack.

"Megan, I'll be there after school to pick you up. Logan, is anything special happening this afternoon, or do I pick you up right after school, too?" I ask, driving through the hillside neighborhood, a swirl of winding dirt roads, and colorful ranchers (ranch homes).

"Just the normal time, Mom." Logan runs a hand over his unruly auburn hair; the cowlick over his right eye has aggravated him for years, and it's not cooperating this morning. "I do have Scouts tonight," he mentions, an afterthought, pulling down the visor to look at his reflection in the mirror. Monday through Friday nights, there's always an activity of some sort—Boy Scouts, Girl Scouts, soccer, basketball, cheerleading, and Civil Air Patrol; we try to be out of the house—and away from Greg—as much as possible.

"I haven't forgotten." We reach the stop sign where our development meets the paved road. "I think you're out of time, honey. Here comes your bus."

"See ya," he says and puts up the visor with a snort of disgust. Logan opens the door, waits for the high school bus to come to a full stop, and then waves as he leaves. Meg's bus is right behind his. We get out of the car, and I hug her tight.

"Love you, Mommy," she says as I hold her.

"I love you, precious girl. Have a great day!" I walk with her across the road to help her up the bus's steps, then wave from the stop sign until the bus is out of sight.

I get back in the Buick, drive, and there's our beige rancher with forest green trim at the very top of the hill. The mountain views are awesome, but it's too far from the main road to expect the kids to walk to the bus. Greg disagrees, but I'm the one to drive them, so it's none of his concern. *Just one of many things we don't agree on, really*—However, I rein in this train of thought, bitterly acknowledging to myself that that list could go on forever.

I brush my teeth and hair, put on makeup, put a load of whites in the washer. Then I slide out of the Crocs, step into my Nikes, grab a NutriGrain bar, and I'm off again. I need to get to work before nine.

I arrive at The Flower Basket in time to turn the radio on, settle in to hear the nine o'clock broadcast of obituaries. Only two today, but they're going to be big—young people always get lots of floral arrangements. One was a sixteen-year-old girl with parents, siblings, grandparents, and the other was a thirty-eight-year-old construction worker with a wife and three kids. *Definitely going to be busy*, I think, bracing myself when the phone rings as if on cue.

Brittany, long-time friend and business partner, comes in at ten to find me surrounded by buckets of daisies, baby's breath, carnations, roses, and lilies.

"Good morning," she says, walking past me to hang up her jacket in the backroom where we keep our silk flowers. I can smell the jasmine notes of her favorite perfume.

"Morning," I answer, noticing her long red hair is gone. "Wow! You look great, Brittany"—her petite frame, heart-shaped face, and blue eyes accentuated by this new pixie style.

"Thanks," she pats her hair self-consciously. "Still feels strange, but I think I like it." Brittany pauses next to me to admire the three completed funeral baskets in front of my workstation. I can tell by her expression—one upraised ginger eyebrow and slightly pursed lips—that she also sees the stack of orders to be filled clasped by a clip on the wallboard behind me. "Busy already," she remarks over her shoulder, tucking her purse on the shelf under the cash register next to mine. "Who died?" She's lighting the Country Home scented Yankee candle on the cluttered desk next to the glass doors of the flower cooler. *I meant to do that,* I think.

"One of the Kitzmiller brothers had a heart attack and died, and Tammy Schell was in a car accident last night with her boyfriend. He survived—she didn't," I reply, making a big yellow bow for the next funeral basket for Tammy. I can't help but think that she was only three years older than Logan; he probably knew her. I push the bow's wooden pick into wet Oasis, add the greens, creating the shape of the design before adding flowers.

"The funeral homes called. We've got both casket sprays, but I didn't want to start them until you got here," I add, but Brittany is already answering the phone. Her sweet disposition and impressive business acumen make her the perfect partner for me; she handles the phone, sends out the monthly bills to our customers, keeps track of inventory and payroll. She leaves all the flower choices, wedding planning, and floral designs to me. I love the creativity of this job, but the math and money are a pain; this arrangement works well for us.

Mrs. Kitzmiller comes in to order her husband's casket spray and three casket pillows from her children. She can't be much older than I am, but the past twenty-four hours have aged her. There's anguish in her amber eyes; the dark circles beneath them, tearstains, and her crazy hair tell their own tale. Poor woman: she is living a nightmare, waiting to wake up. I empathize—ever since I married Greg, I've been living a nightmare of my own creation.

Mr. Kitzmiller had been a hunter; his wife wants me to do a casket spray that looks natural—"outdoorsy"—and features a large figurine of a ten-point buck at its center. "I'll make it beautiful," I assure her, accepting the deer figurine she chose from the shelf. "I'm so sorry for your loss, ma'am. Brittany will ring up your purchases," I say, herding her to Brittany to complete the sale. I hear her begin the sad tale of Mr. Kitzmiller's demise and Brittany's respectful responses. We've seen it before: she has to keep repeating the story, so she believes it herself. Disturbing thoughts filter through as I walk to my workstation, turn on the hot glue gun: Would I mourn Greg's death? He's older than Mr. Kitzmiller; it could happen. I've lost respect for Greg. He never takes responsibility for his actions; he won't learn to read; we have nothing in common except our daughter —our daughter, the one I was supposed to die birthing, but I survived. I don't even like him. I put together the frame for a casket spray while planning which flowers to use for Mr. Kitzmiller's spray. I decide on white roses, purple liatris, white wax flower, yellow carnations, and gold saladago. The silver bell on the door jingles half-heartedly as Mrs. Kitzmiller leaves.

Minutes later, I'm just finishing the white roses on Mr. Kitzmiller's spray when I hear the bell clang as the front door slams. Mr. and Mrs. Schell have arrived. If grief could take a masculine and feminine form, this is what it would look like—sobbing faces, barely upright, one false move and both of them would topple over. Brittany and I make eye contact; I send a silent plea for help with my eyes. I'm speechless, their pain contagious. Brittany—bless her—takes action. With a box of Kleenex, she walks up to the couple, gives a hug and a sympathetic smile. Within a few minutes, the Schells are ready to speak to me about what Tammy's casket spray should look like. They want pale pink gladiolas, dark pink roses, purple iris, baby's breath, and Tammy's big white teddy bear with a pink bow, which they brought with them in a plastic Walmart bag. Brittany runs their credit card as I hug Mrs. Schell. I know who Tammy is now—her little brother plays soccer with Logan. Emotion overwhelms me; tears fall as I take the teddy bear, and return to my workspace.

Brittany and I don't take a lunch break; we're too busy getting and filling funeral orders—standing sprays, wreaths, flower baskets, dish gardens, peace lilies, fruit baskets, and teddy bears (for the Kitzmiller's children and Tammy's siblings). Our spirits are heavy, weighted with the stories of mourning our customers want— need—to share. That day, there are no celebratory events to add balance; no one orders new baby or birthday arrangements.

By four o'clock, all the orders are filled, and I'm emotionally drained.

"You can leave; I'll lock up," Brittany calls, turning off the red neon 'open' sign in the window.

"I'll take you up on that offer," I answer, closing the Teleflora software and prompting the end-of-day report to print. I grab my purse. "You and Ernie doing anything tonight?"

"I don't know," Brittany replies, standing next to me, reconciling the register's daily totals. "Something romantic. Maybe a candlelit dinner and a movie. I want to relax." She's counting out change as I reach the front door. I'm counting the differences in our marital relationships.

"Enjoy your evening. See you tomorrow." I shut the door behind me, walk to my car.

Megan's waiting in the front hall of the elementary school when I arrive. She buckles her seatbelt, then we sing songs from the *High School Musical* soundtrack. A few minutes and miles later, we pull up to the high school. Logan, already changed into his Boy Scout uniform, gets in the front seat after his sister begrudgingly moves to the back. Since we don't have time to go home, we stop at Arby's to eat a quick dinner. I eat a roast beef sandwich with Horsey Sauce, and the kids annihilate their hot ham-n-cheese sandwiches. Afterward, we head to Grace United Methodist where Logan's troop meets.

"Are you guys coming in tonight?" Logan asks as I park the car on the quiet, tree-lined side-street. The stained-glass church windows, illuminated from within, cast a subtle glow over the tidy landscaping below. The scene reminds me of a Thomas Kincaid painting.

"Yes, we'll come," I decide out loud. And we all get out of the car. Once inside, the fellowship hall is full of parents, all talking about either the sudden death of Ryan Kitzmiller or the tragic death of Tammy Schell.

"I've changed my mind," I say to Logan before he is called away to join his Scout buddies. "I'll be back to pick you up, okay?" Unfazed, Logan wanders off with two of his best friends as Meggie, and I escape.

"Where to now, Mommy?" Megan asks from the front seat. "To the park, honey," I reply. "I'll walk the track, and you can play on the slides or walk with me."

The park is the right choice. The soft, rhythmic lapping of the nearby river soothes me; the continuous breeze tickling the leaves of the maple trees and the sound of blue jays and chickadees twittering connect me to life. Meg plays on the playground equipment that sits in the center of the track while I absorb the sunshine, breezes, birdsong, and flowing water, plugging into nature the way a phone is recharged from a wall socket.

"Daddy!" I hear Megan shout, and, like a kite struck down by lightning, my happy mood is destroyed. *Damn! What's he doing here?* Greg walks toward me.

"I saw your car on my way home. Everything okay?" he asks, falling into step beside me. He's only a couple of inches taller than I am, but his legs are longer, and he shortens his steps to keep pace with me. Megan runs up, hugs him, then runs back to the center of the track, content to play again.

"Everything's fine." But I don't make eye contact. "I just didn't want to stay at Scouts tonight," I add, shrugging.

A jay squawks at us from a nearby aspen.

"A school buddy of mine died last night. His wife is screwed," Greg comments after a few minutes of awkward silence. "He didn't have life insurance or any plan for them. They have three kids, too," he continues, filling the void between us.

"Sorry about your friend. Two young people had funerals today. I was really busy at the shop." We walk around the gravel track a couple of times in silence. We don't touch or look at one another, but we walk in tandem. We're like characters from *The Wizard of Oz*—he's the brainless Scarecrow, and I'm the heartless Tin-man, both stuck on a circular yellow-brick road.

Greg clears his throat. "I don't want that to happen to us."

"What?" I'd been daydreaming—wishing I was Glenda, the Good Witch, floating away in a shimmering bubble.

"Dying unprepared—the kids, unprotected. Maybe we need to purchase grave plots..." He's still talking, but I'm not listening. And I've stopped walking. I can't take another step; my thoughts are racing. *Pick out grave plots! I've been stuck with you for years, and now you want me to be trapped next to you—in the ground— for eternity?*

Greg realizes I'm no longer walking, stops, turns back to face me.

"What's wrong?" he asks, a look of confusion on his rather large face. He's balding early, with a large, bare circle on top of his head. What hair he has is dark brown mixed with gray, but he's only forty.

"Cheri? What's wrong?" he repeats, beside me now, touching my cheek with his work-callused fingertips. I pull away.

"No. Definitely, no," I shake my head, my voice hard and cold, an iceberg. I turn around, walk toward my car. "Meggie, come here, please! We need to get Logan," I say, my voice raised. I hear the gravel crunching behind me; I don't turn. "I'll be home in a bit," I say to no one.

"Mommy, can I ride with Dad?" Megan asks from behind me. I turn, smile, see her standing next to Greg, both the recipients of a shared ancestor's upturned, freckled nose. She might have his nose, but she's my girl, and she'll be worried if she senses my mood.

"Sure, honey," I answer, reaching out to hold her little hand in mine. "I'll be home as soon as I get your brother. Pick out your outfit for tomorrow, lay it on your dresser, and start your bath. I'll be home in time to help you wash your hair." I bend, give her a quick kiss, then open his truck door for her. Megan climbs up in the black leather seat and buckles her seatbelt as Greg gets in the driver's side. He says something to me, but I just wave and open my car door.

Standing on asphalt, I watch him leave. Perhaps I should love him, but I don't. *It's time to end this farce.* I see his red brake lights, watch his white Dodge Ram turn right on the highway from the park exit, speeding up to match the flow of traffic. *I'm filing for a divorce tomorrow.* I slide into my car, start its engine. Resolved to explore a new path, I turn left.

TWENTY-THREE

ONCE UPON A SPA

Dione Laufenberg

The girls were off to school. I stood in my walk-in shower, feeling the warm water beating down my back. I am always the last one to shower. I am generally the last person to do most things in my household. I brushed and styled my daughter's Giana, six, and Misha, three, hair, then stood on the side of the stool and jostled the toothbrush in all the hard to reach spots and watched as the chunks of waffle bits from their breakfast adhere to my side of the freshly cleaned double vanity. My husband of 12 years, James, had walked our eldest Giana to the bus stop and dropped our youngest daughter Misha off at preschool on his way to worked. My schedule for the next weeks was nothing like it had been before the sale of the spa business. I spent those days living the good life: I would jump on my Mindbody app, book morning yoga classes, schedule a consultation with a hot tub dealer, and be interviewed for the Sun Prairie Neighbors' Magazine about my family and career moves.

I had sold my business, a boutique day spa on the Eastside of Madison, Wisconsin. It had been a big accomplishment for me, building the space out, hiring staff and finding a following amongst loyal clientele. I had a core team of talented and intuitive therapist, we were known for our Rendezvous Couple's Massage, but I had also had my fair share of drama. I was walking away from the deal with a profit, solid friendships, and high ratings on Yelp and Google. It was a brand that would continue beyond my ownership with a new owner with fresh ideas and the willingness to invest in expansion. I was proud of how much I had developed the company, sad that I wouldn't see my co-workers as often and unsure of what I would do with my new-found freedom. I had morphed into a list of obligations to everyone else, my needs never making it on the list. I was rushing through my life, overbooked and not present in the moment. I wondered to myself how I might reward myself for this major triumph.

I had inherited the caretaker, put-myself-last trait from my mother, yet in many ways, I was determined to resist it. She loved to entertain and was always helping her family and friends. She was a host who had Tupperware, Avon and Mary Kay parties. She ran the kitchen committee for the church, helped to host annual gatherings for New Year's Eve and the fourth of July. We lived near Warner Park which held Rhythm and Booms, a huge fireworks show. We had prime parking. By the end of the night, people would be begging to pull in on our grass, it would be crowded from visitors from surrounding cities. It was hands down my favorite holiday! The smell of pine sol giving way to fried chicken and ribs as mama prepared for our family and friends.

I admired her. Person could rely on her. Widowed and from the projects, she raised five kids when my father was murdered at the young age of 34; she persevered. She moved our family to Madison encouraged by my Uncle Bubble's advice that it was safe place to live and would offer us more opportunity. She went to school and got certified in Phlebotomy and worked at St. Mary's hospital until she retired in 2016. She never hesitated to lend a hand, ear or even a couple dollars. Many photos of her display her in the kitchen preparing mass quantities of food, the phone cord dangling from her ear. She might have been counseling her drug-addicted sister, arranging for a ride for her delinquent grandson or suggesting a game plan for her unemployed girlfriend who needed to get her shit together.

Mama found love again and married pops, a southern man with long hair he wore in a jerry curl. Pops loved to wear leather and suede, and he designed his own clothing and accessories. His pieces were reminiscent of what Prince or Rick James would wear on stage. He dabbled in ownership and sold his clothing and accessories at a flea market when he wasn't working 2nd shift at the bakery. He smoked a pipe, and he smelled like tobacco and Old Spice. He brought his traditional family values with him from Rosedale, Mississippi and when we returned to his hometown each summer, it felt like we had stepped back in time. Stray dogs roamed the streets, the candy lady sold slushies and huge pickles in Styrofoam cups from her back porch which stood on stilts. I once got ringworm from a litter of Kittens I found underneath Grandma Josephine's porch.

When Pops moved in, he would conduct family meetings and sit at the head of the table, dictating the rules and chores us kids would need to follow in his household. Any response, suggestion or question would be considered "talking back," and questioning adults was plain disrespectful. I was happy mama had found love and security, but I was dismayed to see my resilient matriarch sit quietly as this new addition to our family declared how we would now function.

When I met James at the Regent St Retreat Bar in 2000, our chemistry was palpable. I was 19 years old with temporary custody of my oldest sister Aretha's ID. James likes to say that he had me after that first encounter, he smiled, showed his dimples and bought me a

Mike's Hard Lemonade, and that was all she wrote, (insert eye rolling emoji).

We had grown up a mere 15 minutes apart. James couldn't recall ever seeing his parents fight, but he also noted an absence of open affection. They rarely discussed conflict in their family. In those early years of dating, we would talk about our upbringings. I was from the city, he lived in the suburbs. I was black, he was white. I had a blended family his was very traditional. We talked endlessly about our hopes and dreams for the future. He loved my big loud family and my mama's cooking. I loved the camaraderie between he and his brother and the warmth in which his family welcomed me. We discussed our childhoods at length, the loss of my dad, the differences in parenting styles, and the traditions we wished to carry on and the traits we vowed to leave behind.

While we differed in our upbringings, our morals and goals were completely aligned. We wanted the same things; to get married, have two to three kids depending on their sex. He was into real estate, I wanted a career in healthcare, helping people. We wanted a nice home and were willing to work hard for a good life.

Little by little, we worked to achieve those goals. Here I was at the closing the chapter to my first career, with no place to report to. I craved a calmer life and wanted to focus on my kids while they were still young.

So, the question lingered…how could I commemorate this moment? Entrepreneurs don't usually get pats on their backs or acknowledgment of their dedication. Yet for some reason, I wanted a trophy. How was I going to splurge?

"We are not getting a hot tub!" He exclaimed. James was so practical, disciplined, and fiscally responsible. It should come as no surprise that he would see a hot tub as a waste of discretionary income.

I had always been the social coordinator, event planner and celebration specialist in our relationship and eventually for our family. This was my heritage. My party planning was thorough. I thought of the themes, decorated and pinned recipes. I was into the details; I was the head of the fun department! Even the parents were delighted last year when the farmer showed up at Misha's third birthday party with piglets and bunnies.

Our wine-tasting parties were also a hit, each couple brought a bottle of their favorite white and red. We concealed them in wine bags upon their arrival. Then threw $10 into the winner's pot and grabbed a score sheet. We sipped at stations set up with a list of descriptors placed to facilitate conversation about the taste; buttery, complex, smoky, flabby, and earthy. I placed palette cleansers between each station. No one could fathom doing math after all that wine, but James jumped on his desktop and summed the scorecards at the end, so we could crown the winner.

I brought up the hot tub one night over dinner with friends, hoping to recruit some support for my hot tub mission. Sadly, the consensus amongst them was that it would be a pain to maintain, it would drive up the utility bills, and it would be a commodity that would lose its appeal and eventually become an eyesore in the backyard.

My husband had made the executive decision that we would pay down a chunk of the mortgage on our newly built home within days of closing the spa's sale. This was not a financial decision I disagreed with, but I did have an issue with him allocating the funds from my company without a strategic conversation. I found out when he sent me a calendar invite to join him at the bank. That move, coupled with the occasional insinuation that I spend frivolously or have a lack of consciousness of our overall budget irritated me. I had developed an appreciation for spreadsheets, quarterly financials, and evaluation of expenses. I knew how to save. I knew when to splurge.

I owed it to myself, a reward a symbol of the accomplishment. What better way to commemorate the accomplishment of successfully building and selling an enterprise, than with a hot tub? A luxury addition to our home with the very same mission as the company I had: to reduce stress and muscular tension. To provide a space to focus inward on oneself, and to wash away the worries. Good pitch?

"I am not going to help you clean it. I will not drain it or deal with the chemicals. I am not even going in it." These were the threats my husband laid out for me when he saw me researching the brands and features online. What happened to the sentiment happy wife, happy life? Had he forgotten he was married to a boss? Hadn't we promised to remain open to each other's wishes? Hadn't we decided not to have one dictator in our household? Hadn't we agreed to an equal partnership? When he said those words, when he gave me his final decision, when he left my opinion out; I heard a challenge in his statement, and I always rise to a challenge.

I diligently continued my research. I talked to owners of tubs. I read articles into the night. I pinned landscaping designs and got quotes. Ultimately, I defied the commands of my spouse and proceeded to order a hot tub. He is not my commander. I hired an electrician to come and wire it, I hired a landscaper to add a couple arbor vitae trees for accent.

Giana was on board from the start; she went to the showrooms and walked around with me. She told every kid on the block, her teacher, the bus driver and anyone else who would listen that we were getting a hot tub. I'm sure that grinded James' gears, but I was going to teach my daughter a different lesson on how to use her voice.

After the tub was delivered and installed, I arranged for Giana to have the first hot tub party. We invited a couple of her neighbor friends and schoolmates. They had pizza and changed into their swimsuits. Chanting *hot tub* in unison as I opened the cover and started the jets, the excitement mounted. They played in cascading water fountains, put their faces under the bubbles with goggles on and giggled. They danced to kids bop radio on the Bluetooth speakers, and I made a boomerang giff of them and posted them to Facebook, tagging their moms "the Laufenberg manor just got a little sweeter".

I was confident in my ability to incorporate this lavish amenity into our entertainment lineup. We could use it during our weekly date night and soak our aches and pains away while gazing up at the stars, still talking about those dreams we made in our college days.

It was a solid month after the tub had been delivered before I convinced my husband to enter the water. It was date night; we had put the girls down for bed and opened a bottle of wine. We sunk into the sectional. Under the same blanket arms and legs grazed each other as we watched our favorite sitcom, Scandal. When the show ended, and after a brief period of protest about how he didn't want to change into swim trunks or shower before bed, we stepped into the 102-degree water. I offered him prime seating in the lounger section which stretched the length of his 6-foot-1 height and provided extra jets that hit the hamstrings, calves, and feet. I watched as he shimmied his body into the perfect position, tilting back his head and peacefully closing his eyes. There was no need to gloat as the effervescent bubbles softly pelted us. I tuned out from him and tuned into my body—a temporary and separate peace.

TWENTY-FOUR
AH HA HA

Bar Scott

A summer breeze came through the open windows in my studio on that late night. Peter was already in bed. As usual, we went to bed at different times. He was tired after a day of work, and I was avoiding the loneliness I felt when we lay next to each other. Our marriage had begun to suffer after five-plus years without our son, Forrest. It would be easy to blame it all on his death, but it was more complicated than that. Peter had become more and more interested in bird watching and photography; my concert schedule took me away from home, and when I was home, my writing required solitude that excluded him. We both traveled a lot, but we went separately most of the time. On one of the few trips we took together to look at Seagulls and Sand Pipers at the Jersey Shore, Peter wanted me to be still and watch for birds with him. I wanted to walk the beach, feel the wind, and get my heart to beat again. We were out of sync. No one was to blame. Our dreams for the future had simply changed. We'd been changed. When we got married, we'd wanted to build a family, a home. Without Forrest and no other children, the differences in our dreams were exposed. He was going one way; I was going another. The love that remained wasn't enough to keep us together.

That warm summer night at our home in Woodstock, New York, I picked up my guitar to play. Within a few minutes, I was playing a pattern I liked and started to hum along. I'm not a great guitarist, so I tend to play one or two simple chords back and forth until I feel comfortable with them. My weakness as a player is often what makes the beginning of a song. It takes me so long to get chords to move smoothly from one to the other that by the time they do, I've started hearing a melody. Once that melody has grown on me, I'm reluctant to change it by adding more chords, so I don't. On that night humming with those first two chords, I sang *I was born in a wishing well*. But that's as far as I got.

Within a year, Peter and I were divorced. I found another place to live in town and started over. Eighteen months later, I left Woodstock for good. By then I'd fallen in love with Brent, the man who would become my second husband. Our life together was about to begin in rural Colorado. The day I got in my car to drive west was a lonely one. No one was there to send me off. I'd been in upstate New York for a long time. Forrest was buried in the ground. His life and death had been headline news in our local paper. Three year old's don't often get cancer. On top of that, I'd been singing in the area for nearly twenty years. I was leaving my friends, my neighbors, my fans, and all the people who had kept me whole while Forrest was alive and after he died. Woodstock was home. Leaving without fanfare felt wrong and odd. It was also the only way I could go. I'd said goodbye to my closest friends the night before. Saying goodbye to the entire community was impossible.

As I traveled east on Route 28 to get on the New York State Thruway, I wrote down the names of every person I could think of in Woodstock so I wouldn't forget them. I wrote until I couldn't think of any more. The list was long. As I added names, the list began to have rhythm. Some of the names were filled-in with details. Brian, the mailman who always said hi to me, was coupled with Hillary Clinton. The three of us share a birthday. Pam was linked to vegan food. Peter to Amy, the woman he would eventually marry. Pam to Gypsy Wolf. Abby to writing, and Dawn to the animals she sat with as they died on the side of the road, cars taking their lives, she not willing to let them die alone. There were so many names, all of them linked to a life I was moving away from. A life I loved. I felt like I was leaving under the cover of darkness, as though I had let an entire community down by not telling them I was going away. For years, everyone in town knew my business. I'd broadcast it widely when Forrest got sick. I'd blogged, I'd written a book, I'd trusted everyone with my heart, and they had taken good care of it. But I was confused about what was right and what was wrong about loving Brent. I couldn't tell anyone what was happening or why it was time for me to go. Our partnership began too close on the heels of long marriages. I didn't want to know who thought it was wonderful and who thought it was shameful. It was all too dear to me to be impacted by other peoples' opinions. Despite twenty years of being cared for and applauded, both for my music and my mothering, I needed to leave without a word.

Westcliffe, Colorado, where I live now, is at 8000 feet in the Wet Mountain Valley just west of the Sangre de Cristo Mountains. This is a white, conservative town, mostly populated by retirees. And there aren't a lot of us: 647 or so in the winter months, a few hundred more in the summer. There are cowgirls, hay crops, rodeos, and concealed-carry. This is not Woodstock. But I felt relief as soon as I got here. I wasn't the grieving mother anymore. I wasn't the singer-songwriter who had to succeed or compete. I wasn't Peter's wife, and I wasn't Forrest's mom. I didn't have to pass his school every day or run into his friends who still asked me about him. As much as I loved all those things, in Colorado, no one knew me. Anonymity gave me freedom.

Over time, though, I began to struggle. With distance, I could see how much I'd relied on the love I was so freely given back in New York. And I hadn't realized how much I needed applause either. My ego was taking a hit. I didn't know if I still wanted to make music, or even if I was a musician at all. I had sung all the time—in the shower, in my car, washing dishes, walking the dogs, then concerts within driving distance nearly every week. When I got to Colorado, I was mute. Had I been singing all those years just to get attention? That was hard to believe, but why had I stopped?

Then every so often I'd take a bath in our bathroom where the acoustics are so good. I'd relax in the hot water and start to sing. I'd hear myself and remember what I loved. I didn't know what to do about it, though. I needed an audience, and I was 1600 miles from the people who knew my voice.

Jeffrey Brown of PBS News Hour interviewed the violinist Joshua Bell. Bell explained the difference between performing unannounced in a Washington DC train station where few people stopped to listen, versus playing at the same station months later when his performance had been advertised. Naturally, many more people stopped to listen when they knew it was Bell playing. Describing the difference, he said, "I need to be heard. I need the attention. It's not about me, though. It's about the music. *It* wants to be heard." I knew what he meant. We want you to listen. We want you to understand. We want you to care about the music we're playing. That's what I was missing in my life.

Two years after I'd been in Colorado I called my friend Abby about the song I'd started back in Woodstock.

"I've got the first line," I told her, "*I was born in a wishing well,* but that's all I've got."

I knew I wanted to write about the dreams I'd imagined for myself, but that's all I could tell her.

"I don't like the idea of you being in a well," she said. "It scares me. How 'bout next to the well? Or beside the well?"

It was just the question I needed.

Imagining myself *in* a well was scary for me too. All I could think was *no one can hear me. They'll never find me down here.* The idea made me sweat. I suppose I could have written about that, but that wasn't what I wanted to write about. When I imagined myself outside the well, everything changed. I could see myself being seduced by the well, wanting to go near it, curious about it, looking down into it, throwing pennies into it, and finally leaning over and singing into it. There was action, and my imagination was excited.

I settled on *near the well*. 'Near' gave me space and a choice about whether to go closer or farther away.

Changing that one word from 'in' to 'near' created a whole new picture in my head. As soon as it changed, I remembered the only well I'd ever cared about. It was at the bottom of a hill next door to my grandparents' house in Bryn Mawr. We used to sled there in the winter. Afterward, my grandmother would give us hot chocolate by the fireplace. That hill, that well, and that living room represented everything good about my childhood. And yet as a kid, I understood that the well at the bottom of the hill was off limits, hazardous. It was hidden under fallen branches. The stone building around it had been painted white many years before. The paint was mostly gone, and the roof was deteriorating, but because I was told to stay away, I wanted to go in.

In my song, the well became a metaphor for my dreams. I thought about all the coins I'd thrown into wells and pools in my lifetime. Wanting something—money, love, a record contract—but more than anything I'd wanted to sing. I'd wanted to sing for the whole world. Not for fame, I thought, but because my voice was a gift that I was supposed to give back. It felt like my destiny. And yet, by the time I was writing the lyrics to my new song, I was mostly unknown despite years of singing in public. I wondered what that said about my voice. Was it really good enough? Had I misunderstood my purpose? Shouldn't the gift of my voice have translated into more success?

As I thought about all of these things, my song began to take shape. I could see myself looking into the well as a young woman, dreaming about what could be. I could hear myself, and it was beautiful—full of reverb, echo and a rich darkness. All I wanted was for someone else to hear me, and that thought made my dreams grow bolder and larger. I began to think about concert halls, bandmates, costumes, and award ceremonies. All of these were dreams I told no one about. Thinking like that was quietly discouraged when I was growing up. Better to go through life without drawing attention to oneself. Writing the lyrics reminded me how real my dreams had been:

> Looked down into the wishing well
> > wished I may when I heard myself.

Wish I may wish I might have the wish I wish tonight.

I'd never shared my dreams with the people who loved me most. I didn't tell my parents. I didn't tell my siblings or my friends, and I didn't tell myself. I didn't want to be prideful or appear overly ambitious. Instead, I told myself if I were good enough I'd be discovered. I'd like to say that I know better now, but I don't. I still feel like if I keep singing someone will hear me. But who that someone is a mystery. Why is one person's ear more important than another's? My dream had been for the powerful one to hear me; the one who could make it possible for a million others to hear me. If I'd articulated this to myself when I was twenty, might I have had a different outcome? If I said it out loud now would it make a difference?

There are lines in my writing that I like better than others. Usually, I like them because they tell me something about myself I didn't know before. The lyric in the bridge of my new song was one of those lines. As I imagined my wishing well, I saw myself going back there over and over again.

> *One-hundred thirty-one buckets of water*
> *drawn from that well*
> *Each sip I took made me thirstier*
> *for more and more of myself.*

I was like Narcissus at the pool, but I was also like any artist who loves what they've created: I wanted more of it, and I wanted to know more about myself.

While I was writing the tag at the end of the song, I learned one more thing about myself. It was an accident like it so often is in songwriting. I was recording while I sang randomly to see if the right words would come out. I started with the first line again: *I was born near a wishing well.* Then I unconsciously added *far away from here.* For the next two lines I thought I'd sung *it feels so far away when I turn and look.* But when I listened back to what I'd recorded I heard this instead:

> *It's not so far away when I turn to look.*

I thought I'd been singing about physical distance, and about the dreams I once had. Instead, I was discovering my dreams were still very much alive.

Admitting to myself that my dreams hadn't gone away allowed me to make sense of the nonsense lyrics I'd been singing over the chorus until then, and which I thought I'd eventually throw out:

> *I sing Ah ha ha*
> *mmm, mmm*

> *Hey, hey, hey*

I'd sung those words unconsciously at first. Now I could see I was making light of my own narcissism, and feeling affection for my younger self too.

While I was making sense of the song, the song was making sense of me.

Ah ha ha

> *I was born near a wishing well*
> > *Overgrown when a red oak fell*
> > *Hidden in the view*
> > *No one else ever knew*
>
> *Looked down into the wishing well*
> > *Wished I may when I heard myself*
> > *Fell under its spell*
> > *All my wishes held*
> > *I sing Ah ha ha, mmm, hey, hey, hey*
>
> *Someone said you can never tell.*
> > *Won't come true you could go to hell!*
> > *Don't know what to do*
> > *If I can't tell you*
> > *I Sing Ah ha ha, hmm, hey, hey, hey*
>
> *One hundred thirty-one buckets of water drawn from that well*
> > *Each sip I took made me thirstier for more and more of myself*
>
> *I was born near a wishing well*
> > *Far away from here*
> > *Ah, it seems so far away when I turn, if I turn to look*

Ah, it's not so far away when I turn, if I turn and look
I sing Ah ha ha, hmm, Ah ha ha,
When I turn, when I look, I sing Ah ha ha
When I turn, when I drink, I sing Ah ha ha
When I turn, and I drink, I sing Ah

To hear Bar Scott sing "Ah ha ha" scan here:

or visit: *https://soundcloud.com/user721225626/ah-ha-ha*

TWENTY-FIVE
BAILA CONMIGO

Linda Ferguson

1. la invitación

All night I was restless. Haunted by the face of my young dance student, her father's quiet presence, the patterned scarf on her mother's head.

Also, I missed the remarkable wind. How all last week it touched my hands, my dress. How it took my hair and sent it flying, sometimes across my face, sometimes up in the air, making me giddy; a child tossed up, then caught by two strong hands.

You felt the wind last week, too. You saw how it was everyone's friend. How it clasped hands with the neighborhood trees and shook their leaves, filling the air with a hint of danger and the thrill of a thousand tambourines, a symphonic cacophony.

No more this week. No more the early October idyll we all enjoyed. The wind is finally stilled, masquerading as the dead, only the dead have more life in them. Even from ashes, *los muertos* rise again and again, as long as someone remembers them. My father's hand patting my back, a red feather in his tweed hat: two images as vivid as the view from my window now; the grass, the fence, the rhododendron.

Last week, I had a buzz of ideas inside my skull, under my skin, caught from the dancing air and trees, the twirling leaves. The wind turned each day into a party of swinging lanterns and new drumbeats, and we were all welcome—the jogger with her waving ponytail, the bank teller blinking in the brilliant light, the girl in shiny black leggings waiting for the bus. Like *muerte*, the wind made friends with everyone.

2. cats and squirrels

In honor of my father, I plant marigold seeds every spring and pray that they'll last until November, that they'll be blooming festival gold and yellow on The Day of the Dead. Would that my brothers and my mother and I could have a *fiesta* each year. That we made sugar skulls and donned shirts embroidered with *azul* threads before parading down the street, tossing marigolds to the other families of the dead.

We all have our ways of grieving. When our father died, I ran to hug my brother, but his arms stayed at his sides. Callie, a writer I know, composed an essay on the pain she felt when she heard of someone killing squirrels for sport. Our former neighbors drooped for weeks after their cat joined the ranks of *los muertos*.

3. perpetual motion

Before the restless night, I taught two classes—tap dance for children, then creative writing for adults. In the writing class, I wrote Spanish words on the board in purple chalk, then my student Janice read them aloud to us with her deep rolling voice. *Mariposa, amarillo, primavera, la playa*—we folded Spanish words into our plain English lines—*cielo, azul, ontoño*.

The words *"los muertos"* lose their chill this time of year. On doors we see grinning skeletons, knees hiked up as if they were jigging, suggesting death is a kick. In the window of the fair trade shop are displays of miniature bride and groom skeletons; an entire band of bones playing trumpets and drums; the fancy Catrina, in her fine red dress, her skull wreathed with flowers, her mouth open, as if she were about to sing. Diego Rivera painted her with Ollin, the symbol of perpetual motion, on her belt buckle.

When Selena, my young student, first took a dance class from me, she clutched her mother's sleeve, reluctant to move, to join our circle. Now she always wants to be first to try a new step. Selena, dressed in tumbled pink and purple and red; long, loose hair—*negro*.

4. *humo*, swoon

In Central Oregon, where Callie lives, our friend the wind has been carrying the ravenous flames on its back. While some animals are killed or injured, others discover ways of adapting, burrowing in the ground or fleeing the smoking forests.

The Spanish word for smoke, *humo*, transforms when it refers to cigarettes or cigars—*fumada*. When Janice read the purple chalk words in her rich voice, I held my breath and thought of an English word: *swoon*.

5. *mañana*

Last week my husband and I sat outside in the wind, our feet perched on the porch railing. We each held a drink in our hands, the ice cubes clinking inside our glasses, the leaves and the branches all waving in the wind, and I was secretly happy that it was cool enough again to wear my green sweater—*verde*, as Janice said.

Selena's quiet father wears sweaters and a long, graying braid. He grows a thin beard on his chin; a touch of smoke, a touch of frizz. At the end of class, he waits while Selena hovers beside me, ready to be first in line for the sticker ritual. The flower, the frog, the fairy, the sun, the cat—she knows which one she wants.

"Tomorrow," Selena announces, "I'll see my friend. Tomorrow, I'll see my grandma." Tomorrow and tomorrow and tomorrow: Selena has many plans.

6. *lo siento*

Some people inspire us. How I wish I was one of them. Once Del, the manager of our apartment where we were living, responded to our perfunctory, "Hello, how are you?" with a genuine affirmation: "Good to be alive!" Oh, all these years later, how I want to be a Del, to glimmer, to glow, like the golden wind.

I'm on the eve of turning 50 and ashamed of my prickly, petulant history. Today, sick with allergies and feeling befuddled in the behemoth grocery store, I stood in the middle of the aisle fumbling through the crumpled papers in my purse, looking for coupons. When a young mother asked me to move my cart, I hopped aside like a startled bird then thought, *"Fuck you."* Once, when I was a girl, my mother sent me to walk the dog when I wanted to stay home and read. Feeling sorry for myself, I yanked hard on the dog's leash and made him yelp.

Lo siento, I'm sorry.

7. Selena forever

If you Google "Selena" you'll see: Selena Gomez, Selena, Selena Gomez pregnant, Selena Gomez bikini, Selena Gomez twitter, Selena Gomez and Justin Bieber.

The lone "Selena" was Selena Quintanilla-Pérez, a singer who was born in 1971 and murdered in 1995 by Yolanda Saldivar, the president of her fan club. At one vigil, an estimated 60,000 people gathered to grieve the singer.

She was called the "Queen of Tejano Music" and "the Mexican equivalent of Madonna." The story of her life was the basis of a musical: *Selena Forever*. David Byrne and Selena wrote a song called "God's Child," which included an invitation to dance: *Baila conmigo*. The day she was buried, an infamous radio personality mocked her, saying that "Alvin and the Chipmunks have more soul." He later apologized in Spanish.

Lo siento literally means "I feel it."

8. *una voz*

El Día de los Muertos is a day of celebration. In Mexico, the banks are closed, and in Guatemala, people fly giant kites. All over the world, the living make elaborate altars, *ofrendas*, in their homes and prepare the favorite foods of their departed loved ones.

If our family celebrated the Day of the Dead, I would make a BLT for my grandmother, who lived to be 101. For my mother-in-law, who grew up on a farm in Scotland, I'd serve biscuits with a pot of Tetley Tea. To honor my father, we'd have handfuls of cookies and bowls of ice cream—the foods he wasn't allowed to eat when he was living.

Some say that the souls of the dead return to earth each year. I think my mother-in-law, who died 18 years ago, returned last spring. I dreamed I saw her wearing a tweed skirt and a cardigan she'd knit herself. She was sitting on a bench inside a bookstore, and I knew that I was finally worthy of being her friend.

Sometimes I think of this: E.M. Forster's life and mine overlapped for eight years. Maud Hart Lovelace was living in California when I first read her book *Heaven to Betsy*. Laura Ingalls Wilder was still alive when my parents met.

"Only connect," our friend E.M. famously said.

I first noticed the headscarf on Selena's mother last June, then forgot about it. A few months before that, I saw a skeletal man limping toward me in the grocery store. He wore a stocking cap pulled over his ears, and his skin was darkened like stained wood. I looked away as I passed him, then felt a light touch on my arm and heard my name in a voice (*una voz*) I recognized. The skeleton-man was my brother's old school friend, Jay.

9. a brilliant career

Last week I played "Mexicali Brass" for my dancers, and Selena said, "My dad plays that song on the guitar."

Idiot! I'm ridiculous and terrified that everybody knows it: A writer who has experienced only the slenderest material success now teaching a children's tap class. How did I get myself into this? Selena's father is a musician. He'll have seen I can't always keep a beat, that I sometimes lose my balance (*pierdo mi equilibrio*) when I stand on the balls of my feet. Do the other parents all suspect I taught myself the *Suzy Q* by watching videos on the internet?

Like Callie's ravenous fires, I was greedy once. When my children were babies, I stayed home with them and worked on my writing while they slept. I had no philosophy. I just couldn't bear to leave, to let someone else curl up on the couch with an afghan and read with them. ("I could eat you up!" my father used to say, trying to catch me and kiss me.)

Our son: The copper hair and creamy cheeks; the two of us singing Frank Sinatra songs in our faded '68 Skylark. "I Get a Kick out of You," "Anything Goes," "Let's Take It Nice and Easy."

Our daughter: A rebel in a striped dress. She fought me and sleep and only succumbed to naps when we were driving. Then I had to carry her inside, the weight of her head on my narrow shoulder, her legs so limp her yellow boots dangled from her feet. Can you see how

I bring out this story as if it were a rare necklace? How I touch each bead with reverence?

Now here I am—almost 50 with a patchwork career, writing and teaching and dancing. I got sick of sitting alone at my desk; I wanted to join the party, so I took classes—first ballet, then tap, then jazz. Since I've started dancing, I've been in ten shows. I like the costumes, the lights, the other performers. An audience! Now my 21-year-old son is teaching me to play the piano. Who knows where that will lead?

10. *purgatorio*

I picture Selena's house looking something like mine. Maybe a couch with an afghan of *rojo* and *amarillo*; some dishes in the sink, a drop of last night's tomato sauce dried on the counter.

All through the restless night I saw images of her family: Selena and her brother, their dark hair and skin ("I'm going to Cuba," Selena tells me)—her father's rain jacket (*verde*). Selena scuffing her tap shoes across the stage. Selena's mother, a scarf where her long hair used to be, but also a smile, startling in its radiance, as alive as last week's wind.

The sudden fire, the freeway accident. For me, these don't inspire the same fear as the purgatory of treatment: x-rays and biopsies, hopes for survival tainted by operations. Choices, choices, choices: the headscarf or the wig. The weight loss and the crooked walk, then, for the less fortunate, sips of Ensure, morphine and the unflagging virtue of the hospice.

I'd forgotten about the scarf, but in the night, it rises.

11. tick-tick-tick-tick-tick

All through the quiet, windless night an element of discomfort, as if I was straining to keep my balance, with half my body poised over the edge of the mattress. Or maybe as if a light was shining on my closed eyelids, or like I was on an airplane, and knew a stranger might pass my seat and see me sleeping with my mouth open.

My parents used to despair that I was a mouth breather. I had no idea what the problem was, except that it gave my brother ammunition to mock me. I slept under a white bedspread printed with flowers bigger than my hands; even back then they looked old-fashioned, deep red, the color of azaleas. At night I clutched my favorite doll—a cowboy with orange yarn hair and a red gingham shirt with a blue heart glued to it. "Teddy Ticker" he was called because inside his chest was some kind of mechanism that went tick-tick-tick-tick-tick when you moved him. A birthday present.

Selena just turned seven. In a few weeks, I'll be fifty. No black balloons for me. I want extravagant bouquets: roses, zinnias, and chrysanthemums; a big pot of azaleas.

12. the family of *los muertos*

Beneath my head of thick long hair is skin, beneath the skin a skull—not made of sugar, but of bone—inside the skull is a hive of hidden thoughts, and voices that speak in twitters and whines and booming ha-ha's, but also soothe and roll and urge me to wreath myself in gold and extend my hands to the family of *los muertos,* meaning you and my children and Selena, Callie and my husband, Janice and Jay, my mother and my brothers: everyone.

13. balance

is the same word in English or Spanish. It means to be swept up with living while waltzing with the dead.

· · ·

"Baila Conmigo," was originally published in the 2013 issue of Perceptions Magazine of the Arts.

THE AUTHORS

Karen Ackland is a writer in Santa Cruz, California. Her work has appeared in *Catamaran Literary Review, Story Quarterly, The Summerset Review, Salon,* and the *Ploughshares* and *Prairie Schooner* blogs. She holds an MFA in Fiction from Pacific University in Oregon.

Patricia Byrne is the mother of three. Her oldest son, Kurt, is in long-term recovery. She is the creator and editor of the blog *Heroin. Stop the Silence. Speak the Truth.*

Dawn Cogger is a retired nurse, grandmother, and retreat leader. She has been published in *Presence*, an International Journal of Spiritual Direction. She lives in North Carolina with her husband, spending their summers in Wisconsin.

Cate Dicharry graduated from Lewis & Clark College in Portland, OR with a BA in Political Science in 2003. She went on to earn an MFA in Creative Writing from the Low Residency Program at the University of California, Riverside, and now lives in Iowa City with her husband and two small sons. Cate works at the University of Iowa International Writing Program. Her debut novel, *The Fine Art of Fucking Up*, was published in 2015.

Linda Ferguson is an award-winning writer of poetry, fiction, and essays. Her poetry chapbook was published by Dancing Girl Press. She teaches creative writing classes for adults and children https://bylindaferguson.blogspot.com.

Elena Harap grew up in Nashville, Tennessee. She holds an MFA in Writing from Vermont College of Fine Arts. Her poems and essays have appeared in *Jewish Currents, Amoskeag, Anthropology and Humanism, Poetry Porch, Mount Hope, Boston Small Press* and *Poetry Scene*. A founding member of Boston's The Streetfeet Women, she edited and has contributed to their anthologies *Laughing in the Kitchen* (1998) and *The Bones We Carry* (2009). She lives in Putney, VT and teaches in Roxbury, MA.

Duane L. Herrmann, an internationally published, award-winning poet and historian, has held a variety of teaching and other positions and is now retired. A fifth-generation Kansan, with Native and European ancestry, he writes from, and about, these perspectives. His history and poetry have won awards and been translated into several languages. Collections of short stories and of historical articles are forthcoming.

Amy Lou Jenkins is an award-winning author, editor, and teacher. Her work is inspired by nature and a search for truths. Her essays have been published in dozens of anthologies including *The Maternal is Political* and *Wild with Child*. Her book *Every Natural Fact: Five Seasons of Open-Air Parenting* won a USA Book Award, a Living Now Book Award among others. Her essays have received honors from Literal Latte, XJ Kennedy Award for Nonfiction, Ellis Henderson Outdoor Writing Award, and more. She pens a quarterly review of books for the Sierra Club and writes for children under the name Lou Jenkins. She's taught writing at Universities and workshops for over ten years. Contact her at AmyLouJenkins.com and JackWalkerPress.com.

Catherine Jones is a Midwesterner who has traveled and lived many places, yet sees the world through her upbringing in a college town. Polynesia will always feel like her home. She now lives in the college town of her youth so she can be "tutu grandmother." She works to refine skills in creative nonfiction as she once worked to learn the hula.

Catherine Lanser, a life-long Midwesterner, writes essays and narrative nonfiction. She recently completed her first full-length memoir about her brain tumor and her father's disabling stroke. See more at CatherineLanser.com.

Dione Laufenberg is a Midwest mom of two perfectly blended daughters who inspired her to create Laufty Life (lauftylife.com). She has years of experience in the wellness industry and owned a day spa in WI, an expert in self-care. The blog is a resource for mothers of mixed-race children .

Julia Anne Miller is a doctoral student in Humanities & Culture at Union Institute & University with an MA in Philosophy from Stony Brook University. Her work focuses on language and neuro-divergence. Recent publications include poems about experiencing a traumatic brain injury: "Vacant" in the Kentucky Poetry Society's *Pegasus* Summer/Autumn 2017, and "Twenty-six" and "Uninvited" in the upcoming *Kaleidoscope: Exploring the Experience of Disability through Literature and the Arts* Issue 77.

Cheri Todd Molter of Fayetteville, NC is a recent graduate of Methodist University. Her poems and creative non-fiction essays have been published in *Kakalak 2017, Kakalak 2016,* and *Tapestry.* Her academic research has been published in *Monarch Review* and *Aletheia.* She's currently a Research Analyst at the N.C. Civil War & Reconstruction History Center. She's also happily married and the mother one son, and two daughters

Joanne Nelson's writing appears in anthologies and literary journals such as *Midwestern Gothic, Brevity, Consequence,* and *Redivider.* She writes creative non-fiction, essays, poetry, and commentaries on craft. In addition, she gives presentations on topics related to mindfulness and writing, creativity, and the personal essay. She holds an MFA from the Bennington Writing Seminars and an MSSW from the University of Wisconsin-Madison. More at wakeupthewriterwithin.com.

Colette O'Connor lives and works in the magical Monterey Bay Area of California. Her award-winning essays have appeared in many publications, including the Travelers' Tales "Best Travel Writing" and humor anthologies. She holds an MFA in Creative Writing and has taught at California State University, Monterey Bay. More at coletteoconnor.com.

Julia Older has written poetry, essays, fiction, nonfiction and plays.Literary honors include a First Hopwood Poetry Award from the University of Michigan, Mary Roberts Rinehart Grant for Prose, North Carolina First Poetry Book Grant, Independent Publisher Bronze Poetry Medal, First Daniel Varoujian Poetry Award, several Pushcart nominations, and fellowships to the Iowa Poetry Workshop, Yaddo, and the MacDowell Colony. Her memoir, *Appalachian Odyssey,* recounts her adventure as the 19th woman to walk the 2000-mile Appalachian Trail . Other work by Older appears in Poets & Writers, *The New Yorker, Entelechy International,New Directions, Amazon Shorts, Sisters of the Earth: Women Writing about Nature,* and numerous other journals and anthologies. She writes from her studio in the foothills of Grand Monadnock, New Hampshire.

Judy H. Reedy, aka The Abundalicious Boomer, is a blogger and personal essayist. She has a passion for sharing her personal life lessons dealing with negative self-talk in entertaining ways. Given up for adoption at birth, raised by an unfit mother, and coping with a husband with Alcohol Abuse Disorder, all set the stage. She is writing a collection of personal essays. Find her at judyhreedy.com.

Lois Roelofs holds a master's degree in psychiatric nursing and a doctorate in nursing science. After retiring in 2000 as professor emerita of nursing at Trinity Christian College, she authored a career memoir, *Caring Lessons: A Nursing Professor's Journey of Faith and Self* (Deep River Books, 2010). She blogs at loisroelofs.com. After fifty years of living in Chicago, she and her husband recently moved to Sioux Falls, South Dakota, to be near grandchildren

Deborah Schmedemann spent over three decades as a law professor, writing textbooks on legal research and writing. She completed the Master Track Program in Creative Nonfiction at the Loft Literary Center in Minneapolis and published *Thorns and Roses: Lawyers Tell Their Pro Bono Stories* (2010). She is currently writing a collection of essays for Luke inspired by Keith's life.

Karin Schmidt writes memoir and personal essays, and has been published in newspapers, magazines, and anthologies. She is the past president of the Wisconsin Writers Association. Follow her writing at amillionlittlememoirs.worpress.com.

Bar Scott is an ASCAP award winning singer-songwriter. She has recorded seven albums of original material and performed throughout the east coast. She has also written a memoir, The Present Giver, a workbook for writers called The Lone Writer's

Writing Club, and most recently a chapbook with excerpts from an upcoming book, *Live a Life, Write a Song*, from which "Ah ha" is taken. Her stories have been published in *Stories of Music* (Timbre Press 2015, 2017), *Sun Magazine*, and *She Writes Press* and the *Bycopa Literary Review*. More at barscott.com.

Charlotte Mitchell Smith is a retired Chicago corporate lawyer who now lives outside Spring Green, Wisconsin, with her husband Mike. She enjoys the natural beauty of the Driftless Area of southwestern Wisconsin and likes to read, sew and travel. She enjoys working with her husband to garden and preserve the fruits of their labors in the vegetable garden and orchard.

Annette Van Veen Gippe is a loyal graduate of the University of Wisconsin. She has two beautiful grown daughters and lives in Chicago. Recently retired, she is finally finding more time to write. Her life has taken many paths, and she shares many of them through her writing and participation in local Moth events

Ken Williams worked as a social worker for the homeless in Santa Barbara CA. His writings have appeared in numerous publications both in America and abroad. He is a disabled combat Marine veteran of the Vietnam War having fought with the 9th Marines better known as the Walking Dead. His latest book is *Fractured Angel*. More at: Kenwilliams-writer.com

PRAISE FOR 'CORNERS'

"If you're feeling stuck, stagnant, or burned out, *Corners: Voices on Change* edited by Amy Lou Jenkins might just be the book for you. With the common thread of change and transformation running through this collection of 25 stories, essays, and other musings on paper, Corners strikes a happy balance between the advice-giving nature of the self-help genre and the storytelling feature of autobiographies and memoirs. It's like attending a group therapy session or a retreat where you get to listen to the wisdom of a diverse array of people—mothers, grandmothers, writers, poets, teachers, travelers, students, singers, combat veterans—who each have a noteworthy story to share.

...there's no denying the book's potential to inspire and move people to reflect and act on their past, present, and future circumstances.

...readers facing a personal crisis may find solace in a story or two from this remarkable collection. For anyone who wants to move on and onward, Corners is a highly recommended read."

Online Book Club

Corners: Voices on Change' is a compilation of memoirs that lead the reader through the process of alienation, diversion, connection, addiction, obsession, absorption, resistance and acceptance. ...I would highly recommend this thought-provoking collection to anyone facing a difficult transition in life.

Reader Views

ABOUT JACK WALKER PRESS

Jack Walker Press specializes in books for adults and children who believe that the best realities are Earth, life, and spirit. And the best virtual realities are books. We partner with you to celebrate just, verdant, thoughtful, and joyful living. Sign up to receive announcements, freebies, and submissions calls at Jack Walker Press Anthologies.

Also by Jack Walker Press:
- Single Scull Rowing for Beginners
- Howie Tootalot in Yellowstone: The Legend of Lake Isa
- Happy and Sad and other Tootalot Feelings

Also by Amy Lou Jenkins
- Every Natural Fact: Five Seasons of Open-Air Parenting